Digital Forensics: A Complete Guide to Modern Cyber Investigation

Concepts, Tools, Evidence Handling, Mobile, Network and Cloud Forensics

Ronaldo Deka
Syed Mufassir Yaseen

Digital Forensics: A Complete Guide to Modern Cyber Investigation

Concepts, Tools, Evidence Handling, Mobile, Network and Cloud Forensics

ELIVA PRESS

ISBN: 978-99993-4-214-8

Cover Design: Eliva Press
Cover Image: www.ingimage.com
Email: info@elivapress.com
Website: www.elivapress.com

This Eliva Press imprint is published by the registered company Eliva Press Global Ltd. part of Eliva Press S.R.L. Publishing Group

The registered company address is: Pope Hennessy Street Level 2, Hennessy Tower Port Louis, Mauritius
Eliva Press S.R.L. Publishing Group legal address is: Bd. Cuza-Voda 1/4 of. 21, Chisinau, Moldova, Europe

Digital Forensics
A Practical Guide
Real-world cybercrime investigations
Step-by-step forensic techniques
Practical tools and case studies
Mr. Ronaldo Deka • Dr. Syed Muffasir Yaseen

Table of Contents

CHAPTER 1

Introduction to Digital Forensics through a Real-World Case

1.1 Introduction: The Invisible Crime Scene

In the traditional times the crimes are being examined by the investigators physical evidence such as the fingerprints, weapons, or footprints. However, in today's scenario the digital world, and crimes often leave no visible traces behind. But, they occur within the computers, and mobile devices, also the networks, that helps creating what is known as an invisible crime scene.

Consider the situation that where a student receives an email that is claiming to be from a bank, and they are asking for urgent verification of the account details. The student may or will clicks on the link, enters all the confidential information, and shortly after, the unauthorized transactions occurs. The email is deleted, and no trace is been left behind.

At this point, the several critical questions can be that:

- How will be the incident be reconstructed?
- Will it be possible to recover deleted data?
- If the attacker can be identified?

The answers to all these questions lies in the field of Digital Forensics, which will plays a crucial role in modern of the cybercrime investigations.

1.2 Understanding the Digital Forensics

The Digital Forensics can also be defined as:

Systematic process of the identifying, preserving, collecting, analyzing, and presenting the digital evidence in such a manner that it is legally acceptable, presentable.

While this definition provides that a formal understanding, and it is more useful to interpret digital forensics in the practical terms. It can also be viewed as the application of the investigative techniques to the digital environments, where the devices such as computers, smartphones, and servers that will act as sources of evidence.

In a simple terms, the digital forensics are transforms raw digital data into the meaningful information that can give us the outcomes of what happened, how it happened, and who was responsible.

1.3 Importance of Digital Forensics in the Modern World

As we know that the technology is growing rapidly and has significantly increased the dependence on digital systems. As a result, the cybercrimes are increasing and have become more frequent and sophisticated. The Activities such as phishing attacks, and the ransomware infections, identity theft, and data breaches are now common and mostly used.

Digital forensics are essential for several reasons:

- It will help us in detecting and analyzing cyber incidents
- It will also enable the recovery of lost or deleted data
- It will provides the legal evidence that can be presented in court
- It will be assists for the organizations in preventing future attacks

Without the digital forensics, it would be extremely very difficult to investigate cybercrimes or to hold the offenders accountable.

1.4 Types of the Digital Evidence

Digital evidence are often refers to any information that can be stored or transmitted in digital form that can be used as tools during an investigation. Unlike the physical evidence, the digital evidence is also be fragile and can be easily be altered or deleted if not handled properly and professionally.

Common types of the digital evidence are include:

- The Emails and attachments
- All Instant messages and chat logs
- The Browser history and cookies
- All the Deleted files and hidden data
- The System and application logs
- An USB and external device activity

An important characteristic of the digital evidence is that it even when data appears to be deleted, but it often remains recoverable and until it is overwritten. This can makes forensic analysis both challenging and very powerful.

1.5 The Digital Forensics Process are

Digital forensic and the investigations follow a structured methodology to the ensure accuracy and the legal validity. The process can generally be consists of the following stages:

1. Identification

The first step is to involve identifying potential and all the sources of evidence. This may include the computers, mobile devices, storage media, or network logs.

2. Preservation

Once evidence is been identified, it must be preserved to prevent any kind of tampering. This will includes and isolating devices and maintaining proper documentation as to known as the chain of custody.

3. Collection

In this stage, the data is been collected and using specialized techniques. Instead of directly accessing the original device, the investigators create a forensic image, which is an exact copy of the data of that evidence.

4. Examination

All the collected data is been examined to extract relevant information. This may include the recovering deleted files as well as, analyzing logs, or identifying suspicious activity.

5. Analysis

Now, the extracted data is to analyzed and to reconstruct the sequence of events. The Investigators attempts to answer key questions such as when the incidents occurred and how it was executed by the culprit.

6. Presentation

Finally, all the findings are been documented in a structured report that it can be presented in Court or organizational settings.

Fig 1.1: Digital Forensic Investigation Process

1.6 Handling the Digital Evidence: Key Principles

It is one of the most critical of all aspects of the digital forensics that is maintaining the integrity of evidence. And any modification to the original data that can be compromise the investigation.

Therefore, all the investigators have to follow the strict principles:

- All the original evidence must never be altered
- It should be always performed Analysis on a copy
- All the actions must be properly documented nothing should miss
- Evidence are must to be securely stored

These are the practices that ensure of the findings remain reliable and admissible in court.

1.7 Introduction to Forensic Tools

Digital forensic and the investigations are very rely heavily on the specialized of tools that assist in data acquisition and the analysis. For some commonly used tools include:

- Autopsy Digital Forensics Platform – Open source tool used for analyzing disk images and recovering files
- FTK Imager – Open source tool used for creating forensic copies of storage devices
- Wireshark – Open source tool used for capturing and analyzing network traffic

These are the tools will help automate complex tasks and provide detailed will insights into digital evidence. In the later chapters, these tools will be explored through practical exercises.

1.8 The Mindset of a Digital Forensic Investigator

Beyond all the tools and techniques, the digital forensics requires also a specific way of thinking. All the forensic investigator must approach all the cases with curiosity, attention to the detail, and the logical reasoning.

Key traits include:

- All the ability to be identify hidden evidence
- We should Analytical thinking to connect the different pieces of data
- Should be Patience in examining the large volumes of information
- All the Objectivity to avoid assumptions

Rather than we should be relying solely on tools, the investigators must also interpret the data and construct in a clear narrative of the incident.

1.9 Case Study: Recovery of Deleted Evidence in a Data Theft Incident

Consider a scenario that a corporate environment is:

An employee is being suspected of stealing the confidential files of the company data before resigning. So, just before leaving, the employee deletes very several files from the office computer and clears the recycle bin. At the very first glance, it can appears that the data is permanently removed, and no evidence remains.

However, the digital forensic investigation tells a different story of the scene, what you think.

Step 1: The Evidence Identification

The investigator must identifies the suspect's workstation as it will be the primary source of evidence. And additional sources may include:

- The External storage devices (USB drives)
- The System logs
- The File access history

Step 2: Next is Data Acquisition

Using the tools like FTK Imager, and a forensic image that of the hard disk is created. This will ensures:

- No changes are made to the original system that was used
- All the data, including the deleted files, is preserved

Step 3: The Examination of Deleted Files

The forensic image can be analyzed using Autopsy Digital Forensics Platform.

During the analysis:

- All the Deleted files are recovered
- The File fragments are reconstructed
- All the Metadata such as file names, sizes, and timestamps are extracted

Even though the files were deleted, traces will still exist in disk sectors.

Step 4: The Timeline Analysis

All the investigator have to builds a timeline based on:

- The File creation and deletion timestamps
- The USB connection logs
- And System activity logs

This will reveals:

- When files were accessed and
- When they were been deleted
- Whether there is any external device that was connected

Step 5: The USB Device Investigation

System logs will indicate that a USB drive that was connected shortly and before file deletion.

Further the analysis shows:

- The Device ID
- The Connection time
- The Data transfer indicators

This will strongly suggests that the files were copied before deletion.

Step 6: A Reconstruction of Events

Based on the evidence that is collected, the following sequence is to be established:

1. The Employee has accessed confidential files
2. The Files were copied to a USB device
3. The Files were deleted from the system
4. Recycle bin was been cleared to hide the traces

Step 7: Lastly Reporting

All the findings are should be documented in a structured forensic report, including the:

- Recovered files
- The Timeline of actions
- Supporting logs and all the metadata

This report also can be used as legal evidence against the suspect.

Key Learning from This Case

- All Deleted data can be recoverable in the field of digital forensics
- Digital actions will always leave traces
- Timeline the analysis is crucial in investigations
- Proper tools and methodology often can reconstruct events

1.10 Summary

This chapter introduced all the fundamental concepts of the digital forensics by using through a practical perspective. It is emphasized all the importance of investigating digital crimes, understanding the different types of evidence, and following a structured of forensic process.

The key takeaway is that the digital forensics is not limited to theoretical knowledge. It is been a practical discipline that is been combines technical skills with the analytical thinking to uncover the truth behind all the cyber incidents.

1.11 Review Questions

Short Answer Questions

1. Define digital forensics in your own words?
2. What is the digital evidence? Provide examples?
3. Why is the preservation important in digital forensics?

Long Answer Questions

1. Explain the digital forensics process in detail?
2. Describe it how a phishing attack can be investigated?

1.12 Practical Thinking Exercise

You may receive a suspicious email containing a link. Then after clicking it, in your system behaves unusually.

- What are steps would you take to investigate the issue?
- What types of evidence you would look for?
- Which are the tools could assist in the investigation?

Multiple Choice Questions

1. Digital forensics is primarily concerned with:
   A. Physical crime scenes
   B. Digital environments
   C. Chemical analysis
   D. Biological samples
   Answer: B
2. Which stage involves identifying potential evidence sources?
   A. Collection
   B. Identification
   C. Analysis
   D. Presentation
   Answer: B
3. A forensic image is:
   A. Compressed backup
   B. Bit-by-bit copy
   C. Screenshot
   D. Encrypted file
   Answer: B
4. Which is a characteristic of digital evidence?
   A. Permanent
   B. Easily altered
   C. Visible
   D. Tangible
   Answer: B
5. Which tool is used for disk imaging?
   A. Wireshark
   B. FTK Imager
   C. Autopsy
   D. Nmap
   Answer: B
6. Digital evidence includes:
   A. Emails
   B. Logs
   C. Browser history
   D. All of the above
   Answer: D
7. Preservation ensures:
   A. Faster analysis
   B. Evidence integrity
   C. Data deletion
   D. Encryption
   Answer: B
8. Which step reconstructs events?
   A. Collection

B. Analysis
C. Identification
D. Preservation
Answer: B

9. Investigator mindset requires:
A. Assumptions
B. Guessing
C. Analytical thinking
D. Ignoring details
Answer: C

10. Deleted data is:
A. Permanently gone
B. Recoverable until overwritten
C. Always encrypted
D. Invisible
Answer: B

CHAPTER 2

The Understanding Cybercrime and Digital Evidence

2.1 Introduction: The Link between the Crime and the Evidence

With the rapid growth of the digital technologies, the almost every human's activities today leaves behind an digital trace. It can be sending an email, or accessing a website, or the transferring files, or the using a mobile application, everything and each actions generates data. When all these actions are associated with the unlawful activities, they it form the basis of cybercrime investigations.

Unlike the traditional crimes, where it is physical evidence such as fingerprints or weapons can be directly be observed, cybercrimes will occur in the virtual environments. As a result, the evidence is not immediately will visible and often exists in the hidden or fragmented forms across the devices and networks.

From the forensic perspective, its focus is not only on the identifying the crime but also on understanding the:

- What are actions were performed
- When all those actions occurred
- Where all the evidence resides
- How the sequence of events are can be reconstructed

Thus, digital forensics can establishes a crucial link between the cybercrime and digital evidence, by enabling investigators to uncover the truth that is behind digital incidents.

2.2 The Cybercrime: Concept and Scope

Cybercrime that is refers to any unlawful activity that can be involves a computer system, or a digital device, or a network. It all may occur in different forms, ranging from of simple unauthorized access to all the complex, organized the attacks targeting an institutions or governments.

From a forensic standpoint, the cybercrime can be understood as:

A sequence of the digital interactions that can violate legal or organizational policies and leave behind the traceable evidence.

Cybercrime are typically involves the three key components:

1. Target – Where all the system, individual, or organization affected

2. Tool – That are medium used (computer, malware, network)
3. Intent – And the purpose behind the act (theft, disruption, espionage)

Understanding all these components will helps investigators to identify where to look for the evidence and how to interpret it.

2.3 Classification of the Cybercrime (Forensic-Oriented Approach

Instead of the studying a cybercrime only from a theoretical classification, it will be more useful to analyze it to base on how forensic evidence is generated.

2.3.1 Unauthorized Access (System Intrusion)

Fig 2.1: Cybersecurity Threats and Data Breach Representation

Failed logon attempts [All users]

Username	Event logged by	Logon type	# of logins
PAW	DC2	Network	4
Administrator	DC1	Interactive	3
administrator	PAW	Interactive	2
bob	WS001	Interactive	2
sql-svc1	PKI	Network	2
Administrator	DC1	Unlock	1
administrator	PAW	Unlock	1
administrator	DC2	Interactive	1
anni	WS001	Interactive	1
eAdministrator	DC1	Network	1

Fig 2.2: Log-Based Detection of Unauthorized Access Attempts

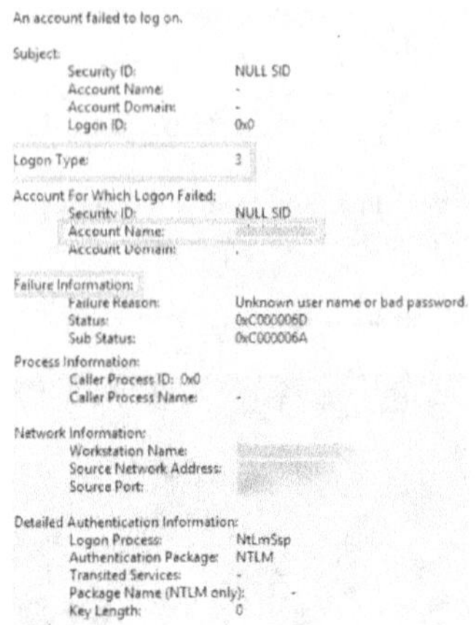

Fig 2.3: Windows Security Event Log Showing Failed Logon Attempt

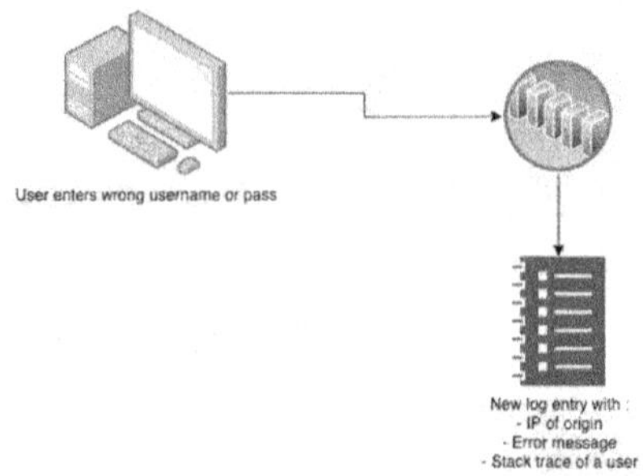

Fig 2.4: Generation of Log Entries from Failed Authentication Attempts

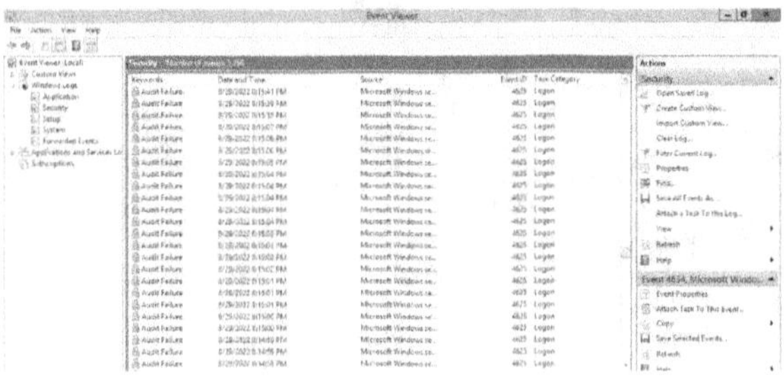

Fig 2.5: Windows Event Viewer Showing Security Log Entries

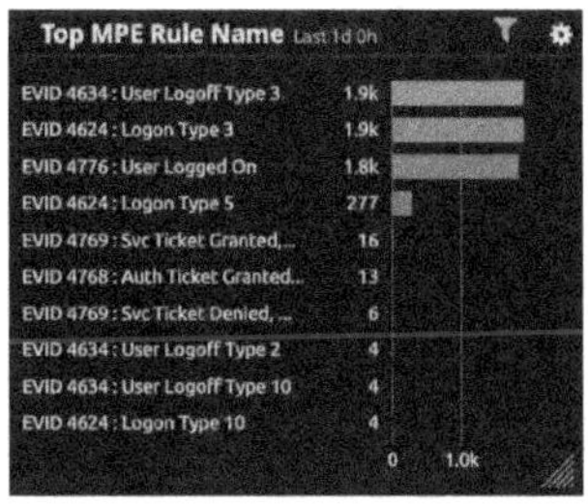

Fig 2.6: SIEM Dashboard Showing Security Event Correlation

Unauthorized all the access occurs when an attacker will gains entry into a system without any permission. This all may involve in password cracking, and exploiting the vulnerabilities, or bypassing all the authentication mechanisms.

From the forensic perspective, and such the activities that is leave behind the several indicators:

- The Authentication logs are showing repeated login attempts
- The Successful login and entries are from unusual IP addresses
- All the Time-based anomalies are in access patterns

These are the traces that helps investigators to determine whether an system was compromised and how the intrusion occurred.

2.3.2 Data Exfiltration (Data Theft)

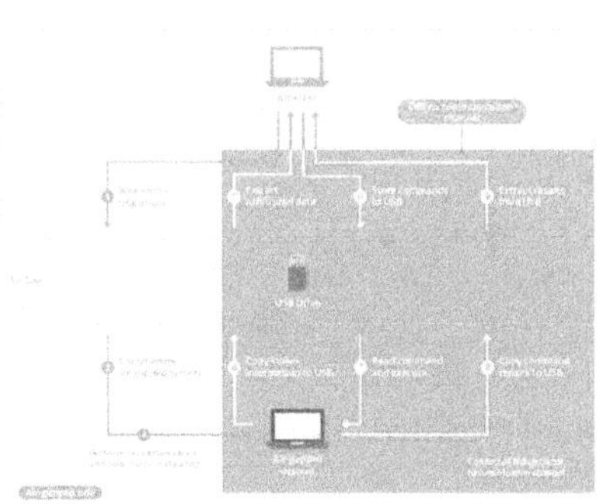

Fig 2.7: Data Exfiltration from Air-Gapped Systems Using USB-Based Covert Channel

Data are exfiltration that involves the unauthorized copying or transfer of sensitive data. This may be performed by the external attackers or internal users.

Key forensic that indicators include:

- The File access and modification logs
- All the Sudden spikes in data transfer
- The Records of external device connections

Even if the data is deleted and afterward, it remnants can be often be recovered by the forensic analysis.

2.3.3 Malware-Based Attacks

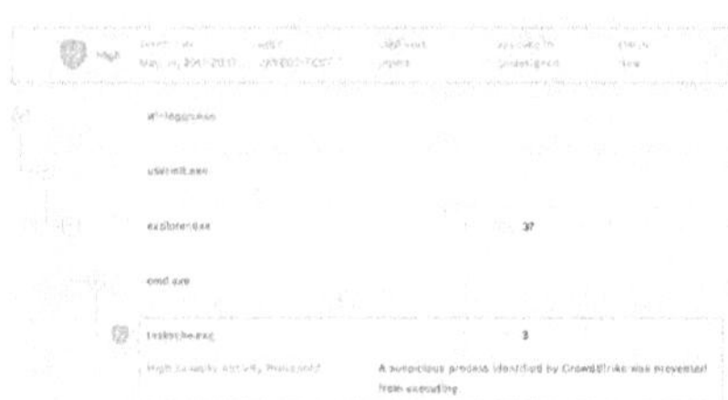

Fig 2.8: Detection and Prevention of Suspicious Process Execution Using Endpoint Security Monitoring

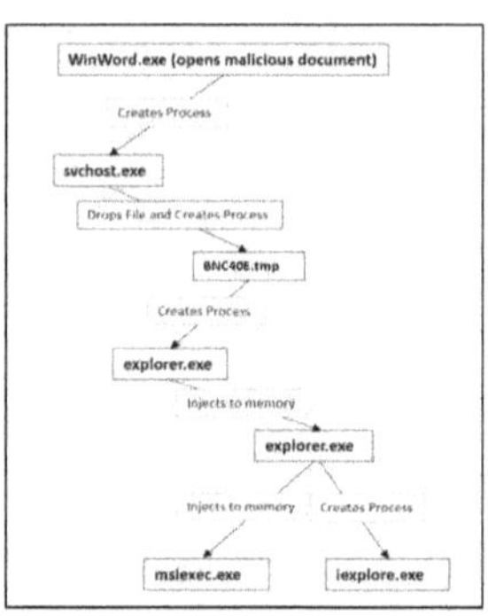

Fig 2.9: Detection and Prevention of Malicious Process Activity in Endpoint System

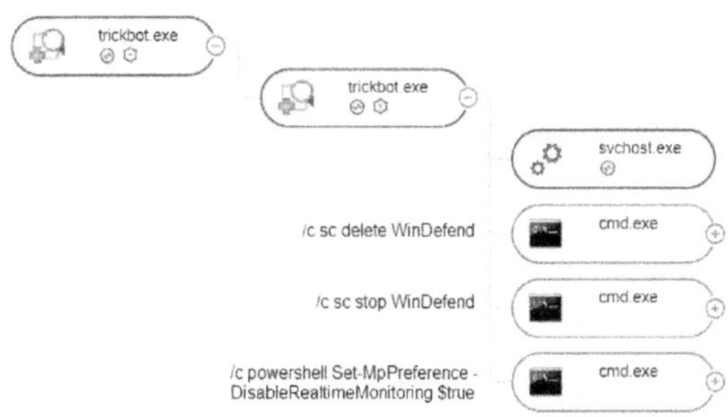

Fig 2.10: Process Tree Analysis Showing TrickBot Malware Execution and Defense Evasion Commands

Malware are to refers malicious software that is designed to disrupt, damage, or gain unauthorized the control over systems.

From an investigative viewpoint, the malware always leaves a traces such as:

- The Unknown or suspicious processes that is running in memory
- The Changes in system files or registry entries
- The Unusual network and communication patterns

These are the indicators that helps in identifying the infection sources and understanding the attacker behavior.

2.3.4 Insider Threats

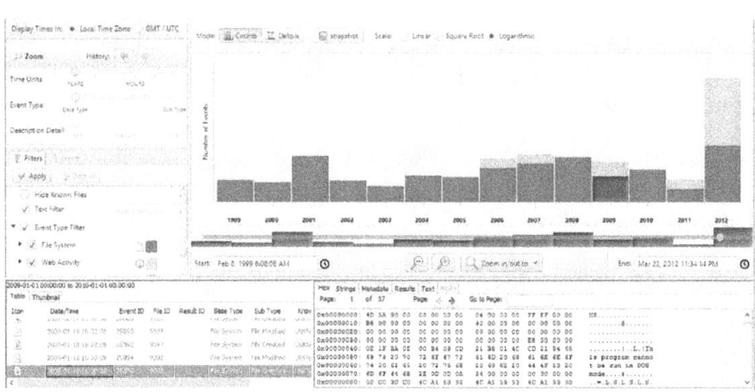

Fig 2.11: Timeline and Hex-Level Analysis of Digital Evidence Using Forensic Tools

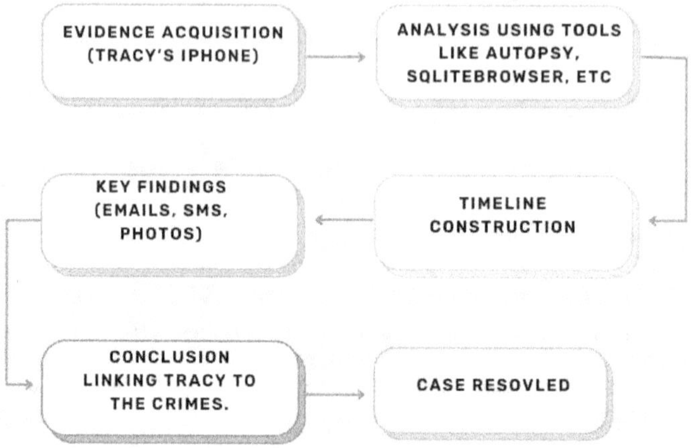

Fig 2.12: End-to-End Digital Forensic Investigation Process

Insider that threats are involve the individuals and who misuse their authorized to access for malicious purposes. These are the cases that are particularly very challenging because of the user already has legitimate permissions.

The Forensic indicators include:

- To access to sensitive files outside normal working hours
- The Repeated or unusual data access patterns
- After Deletion or modification of critical files

Analyzing the behavior patterns that becomes crucial in such an investigations.

2.4 Digital Evidence: Meaning and Significance

Digital evidence that refers to any types of information of the investigative that values is stored or transmitted into a digital form. It will plays a central role in reconstructing the cyber incidents and the supporting legal proceedings.

Unlike the physical evidence, a digital evidence has an unique characteristics:

- It is an intangible and it requires tools for the interpretation
- It can be easily altered or it can be destroyed
- It may be exist in the multiple locations simultaneously

Because of these the characteristics, and proper handling and the analysis are an essential to maintain its reliability.

2.5 Sources of Digital Evidence

Digital evidence are can be obtained from the various sources, depending on the nature of the investigation.

2.5.1 Computer Systems

Computer systems are the primary sources of evidence. They can contain:

- All the Files and directories
- And the Operating system logs
- Also the Installed applications and usage history

These components are provide to insights into user activities and the system behavior.

2.5.2 Network Infrastructure

Network-based are the evidence includes:

- The Router and firewall logs
- And Packet capture data
- Traffic flow records

Such evidence is a useful in tracing the communication between the systems and identifying external threats.

2.5.3 Mobile Devices

Mobile devices are store a large amount of a personal and communication data, including:

- The Call records and messages
- The Application data
- The Location information

They are rapidly increasingly important in modern investigations.

2.5.4 Cloud Environments

Cloud platforms are introduce in the new sources of evidence such as:

- The Cloud storage logs
- The Email service data
- Virtual machine activity

Investigating in cloud-based evidence are often involves additional legal and technical challenges.

2.6 Properties of Digital Evidence

Understanding are the properties of an digital evidence is the essential for proper handling and analysis.

Volatility

Fig 2.13: Memory Acquisition Process Showing RAM Dump for Forensic Analysis

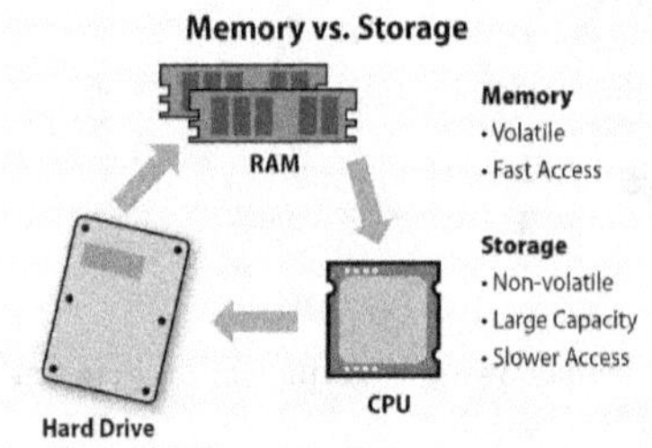

Fig 2.14: Differences between Memory and Storage in Digital Systems

Volatile data will exists temporarily and it is lost when the system is powered off. For Examples include data stored in RAM.

Integrity

Integrity ensures that is evidence remains and unchanged from the time of the collection to presentation. This are the typically verified using hash values.

Authenticity

Authenticity confirms that the evidence is genuine and originates from a reliable source and it is not tampered.

Reliability

Reliability are depends on the tools and the methods used during the investigation. And proper procedures must be followed to ensure the trustworthiness

2.7 Challenges in Digital Evidence Investigation

Digital forensic are investigations face by several challenges:

- Encryption are to protecting data from unauthorized access
- Anti-forensic are the techniques such as data wiping
- Large volumes of data are to requiring analysis
- Legal issues can be different across different jurisdictions

These challenges are to highlight the importance of expertise and the structured of investigation processes.

2.8 Correlating Cybercrime with Evidence

A key of skill in the digital forensics is the ability to the correlate of actions with the evidence.

Cyber Activity	Evidence Generated
Login attempt	Authentication logs
File deletion	File system metadata
USB connection	Device logs
Malware execution	Process and network logs

Table 2.1: Summary of Failed Login Attempts and Authentication Events

This correlation are to help the investigators to reconstruct the sequence of events.

2.10 Summary

This chapter are been explained the relationship between the cybercrime and digital evidence. It is emphasized that the every digital action leaves traces, and these are the traces form the basis of forensic investigation.

Understanding the different types of a cybercrime, sources of evidence, and their properties is essential for the building a strong foundation in digital forensics. The digital evidence can often come from many different sources and such as computers, mobile devices, networks, cloud platforms, and the removable storage media. Each of the sources may be provide useful information when it is not properly collected and examined.

Another important point is that an investigators must also understand the characteristics of digital evidence, including integrity, authenticity, reliability, and relevance. These factors can help to determine whether the evidence can be trusted during analysis and accepted in court proceedings.

In many cases, the successful forensic investigations are very much depend on both technical skills and proper procedure. Because of this, a clear understanding of the cybercrime concepts and digital evidence handling and it is necessary before moving to advanced forensic techniques.

2.11 Review Questions

Short Answer:

1. Define cybercrime from a forensic perspective?
2. What is digital evidence?
3. Explain volatility in digital evidence?

Long Answer:

1. Discuss types of cybercrime with forensic indicators?
2. Explain properties of digital evidence?

2.12 Practical Lab Exercise

Objective: Identify and classify the digital evidence

Scenario:
A system scenario shows:

- The Missing files
- The Suspicious login activity

Tasks:

- Its Identify possible sources of evidence
- Its Classify evidence types
- Its Suggest tools and investigation steps

Multiple Choice Questions

1. Cybercrime involves:
   A. Only hacking
   B. Digital systems
   C. Only fraud
   D. Only malware
   Answer: B
2. Unauthorized access leaves:
   A. File content
   B. Login logs
   C. Images
   D. Videos
   Answer: B
3. Data exfiltration means:
   A. Data backup
   B. Data theft
   C. Data compression
   D. Data encryption
   Answer: B
4. Malware affects:
   A. Only hardware
   B. Software and system behavior
   C. Only networks
   D. Only RAM
   Answer: B
5. Insider threat involves:
   A. External attacker
   B. Authorized misuse
   C. Firewall
   D. Encryption
   Answer: B
6. Volatile data resides in:
   A. HDD
   B. SSD
   C. RAM
   D. USB
   Answer: C
7. Which is NOT a source of evidence?
   A. Network logs
   B. Cloud
   C. RAM
   D. Printer ink
   Answer: D
8. Integrity ensures:
   A. Speed

B. Data unchanged
C. Encryption
D. Compression
Answer: B

9. Reliability depends on:
A. Tools and methods
B. Internet speed
C. Storage size
D. RAM
Answer: A

10. Cybercrime components include:
A. Target
B. Tool
C. Intent
D. All
Answer: D

CHAPTER 3

Evidence Handling, Disk Imaging and Chain of Custody

3.1 Introduction

In digital forensic the investigations, the value of evidence lies not only in what is discovered but also in how the data is handled. Digital evidence is inherently a fragile and can be easily tampered, intentionally or unintentionally, during this process of collection and analysis. Even the minor changes—such as opening a file or booting a system— both can be modify the timestamps and compromise the integrity of evidence.

Therefore, the digital forensic investigations is required a structured and disciplined approach to the evidence handling. Investigators must also ensure that evidence is collected accurately, preserved, transported, and analyzed in a manner that maintains its integrity, authenticity, Confidentiality, and admissibility.

This chapter also focuses on the principles and procedures that is involved in handling digital evidence, the process of disk imaging, using the write blockers, and the importance of maintaining a chain of custody is very important. These concepts is the backbone of any legally sound forensic investigation in the field of forensics.

3.2 Nature of Digital Evidence

Digital evidence that differs a significantly from the physical evidence in several ways:

- It is the intangible and cannot be physically observed without tools
- It can be easily made duplicated without degradation
- So it is highly volatile in certain cases (e.g., RAM data)
- It also can be altered or destroyed quickly

Because of these characteristics, a special care must be taken when the handling digital evidence. Unlike the physical objects, a digital evidence requires both technical expertise and procedural discipline.

3.3 Principles of Digital Evidence Handling

To ensure that the reliability and admissibility of the evidence, and investigators uses fundamental principles these principles are very important because the digital evidence can be often easily changed, copied, damaged, or deleted if it is not handled properly by the investigator. Even a very small mistake during collection or storage can lead to affect the authenticity of the evidence and can reduce its value during investigation.

In a practice, the investigators have to follow the standard procedures such as proper documentation, secure storage, controlled access, and the evidence integrity and verification. Each of the action can be taken on the evidence and it should be recorded very clearly so that the handling process can be explained later if required.

Another the important point is that evidence handling is not the only way a technical task but also a legal responsibility. For an example, if a storage device is collected without a proper documentation or chain of custody, the findings can be very challenged in court. Because of this, the following evidence are handling principles is essential in an every forensic case that are:

1. Integrity

Evidence must remain untampered and unchanged from the time of collection to presentation. Any modification of the data can be invalidate the investigation.

2. Authenticity

The evidence are very must be proven to originate from the claimed source. Proper documentation and verification methods are used to support authenticity.

3. Completeness

All relevant data are must be collected, and including the hidden, deleted, and the residual data.

4. Reliability

The tools and methods are used and must be scientifically valid so that it can widely accepted in forensic practice.

5. Documentation

Every action can be taken out during the investigation and must be recorded, including:

- The date and time
- what tools were used
- All the personnel involved
- what actions were performed

3.4 Digital Evidence Handling Lifecycle

Handling digital evidence also involves an structured lifecycle that will ensures proper management from the discovery to presentation in the court. In a simple terms, the evidence handling process with the lifecycle and it works step-by-step process followed to manage digital evidence from the moment and it is identified as until the final case conclusion. It is very important because each stage must be completed very carefully to maintain evidence integrity and legal value in the court.

The lifecycle are usually includes the identification, collection, preservation, examination, analysis, documentation, presentation, and it is in secure storage. Every stage has its own purpose, but all stages are being connected and depend with the proper execution of the previous step.

In a practice, if the evidence is collected and correctly but due to poorly documented later, and the investigation may still face the problems. For an example, its extracted and hard drive is an image may contain valuable data, but without a proper records of who has handled it and when, its reliability can be questioned. Because of this, an complete lifecycle must be managed with the consistency and care.

Figure 3.1: Digital Evidence Handling Lifecycle

Figure 3.2: Digital Forensics Workflow

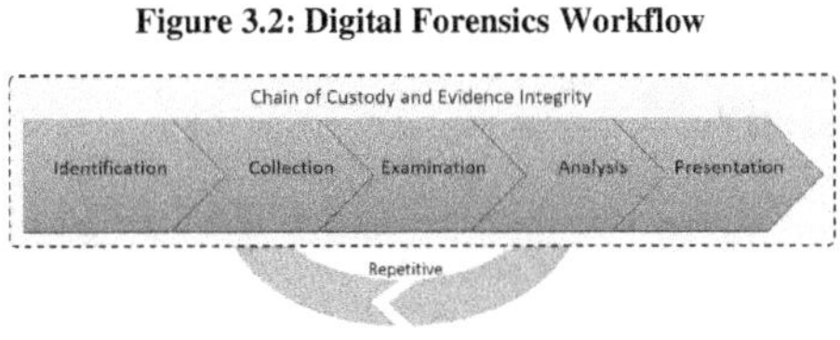

Figure 3.3: Chain of Custody and Evidence Integrity in Digital Forensics

Stages of the Lifecycle:

1. Identification – To Recognizing potential sources of evidence
2. Collection – To Acquiring data from devices
3. Preservation – To Protecting evidence from alteration
4. Examination – To Extracting relevant data
5. Analysis – And Interpreting findings
6. Presentation – To Reporting results

3.5 Evidence Collection and Preservation

Once the evidence is identified, it must also be collected carefully. The Investigators must avoid any action that can be tampered the data. Evidence collection and its preservation are very critical and stages and because digital data can be changed very easily during the handling. A simple action such as an opening a file, connecting a device, or restarting a system can be alter timestamps or it is overwrite the important information. Because of this, the investigators must use safe and in a controlled methods while collecting evidence.

In a practice, the devices should be photographed, labeled, and documented before the seizure. Storage media are often collected using the write blockers or forensic imaging tools so that the original data remains unchanged. Also Proper packaging and secure storage are also necessary to protect the evidence from physical damage, loss, or being accessed by any unauthorized person.

For an example, if an USB drive is found at a crime scene, the investigator have to record it where it was found, seal it properly, and create an forensic copy for the examination instead of directly browsing its contents. This will help to preserve the originality and reliability of the evidence and throughout the investigation.

Key Practices:

- Do not use the operate to the suspect system unnecessarily
- Always Use write blockers when accessing the storage devices
- Create the forensic images before analysis is important
- Maintain all the steps with proper documentation

Preservation ensures that the evidence remains in its original state for the future verification.

3.6 Chain of Custody

Chain of custody is a formal record that is the documents that handling of evidence throughout its lifecycle. It ensures the transparency and accountability. In an simple terms, the chain of custody is an documented history that shows who has collected the evidence, who has handled it, and when it was transferred, and for what purpose it was accessed for. It is an important and because the digital evidence must be remain traceable from the time of seizure to until final presentation in court.

A proper chain of custody should be followed to record a usually includes the date and time, name of the handler, description of the evidence, and what action taken, to transfer details, and storage location. Each and every entry should be clear and accurate so that there is no confusion about the movement of evidence.

Key Elements of Chain of Custody:

- The Unique evidence identifier
- The Description of evidence
- All the Date and time of collection
- Name of person collecting evidence
- Record of transfers between individuals

Date	Time	Handler	Action	Location
10/04/2026	10:00 AM	Investigator A	Collected	Office
10/04/2026	11:30 AM	Analyst B	Received	Lab

Table 3.1: Chain of Custody Log (Evidence Handling Record)

Importance:

- To Prevents tampering
- Ensures the accountability
- It Supports legal admissibility

Without a proper chain of custody, even the valid evidence may also be rejected in court.

3.7 Write Blockers in Digital Forensics

A write blocker is a hardware or software that the device will prevents any modification to the original storage media during extraction process and the analysis. Using Write blockers are very important and because even connecting a storage device to a computer and can automatically change the system files, timestamps, or hidden metadata. In a forensic work, such as changes must be avoided to preserve the originality of the evidence. And because of this, the write blockers are widely used during the evidence acquisition.

In a practice, a hardware write blocker is been placed between the evidence drive and the forensic workstation, allowing that only read access to the device. Software of the write blockers perform a similar function through the system controls and permissions. Both the methods help investigators to examine the data and without writing anything back to the original media.

Functions:

- Always Allows read-only access
- To Prevents accidental writes
- And Preserves evidence integrity

Figure 3.4: Write Blocker Setup

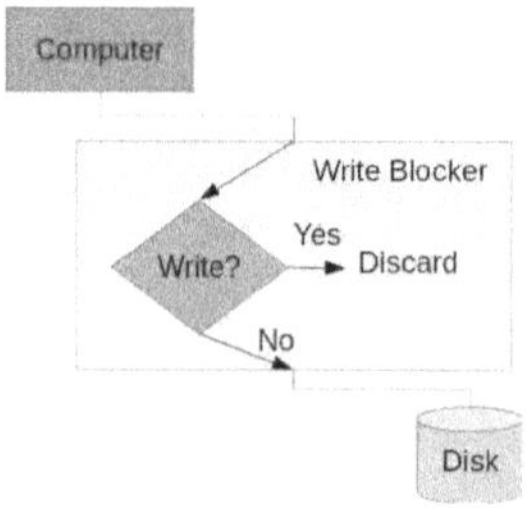

Figure 3.5: Blocker Mechanism in Digital Forensics

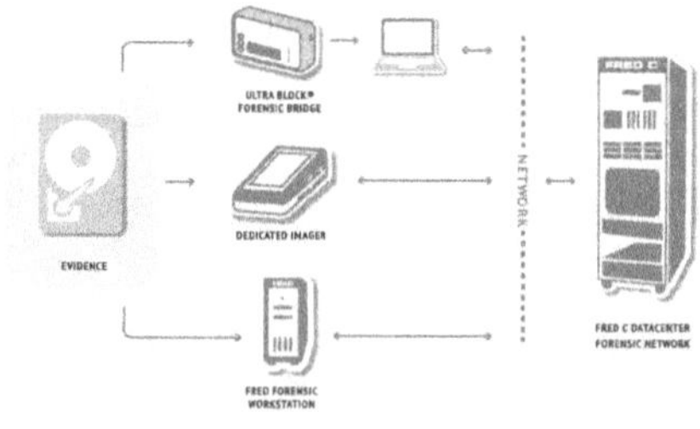

Figure 3.6: Digital Forensic Imaging Architecture / Evidence Acquisition Setup

3.8 Disk Imaging in Digital Forensics

Disk imaging is the process which help us to create an exact duplicate of a storage device. This duplicate, is known as a forensic image that is used for analysis instead of the original device. Disk imaging is one of the most common practices in the digital forensics because it will allow investigators to preserve the original evidence and while still performing a detailed examination. Instead of that it should works directly on the seized device, and analysis is carried out on the copied image file

Tools such as:

- FTK Imager

That is commonly used in the field of forensics.

Types of Forensic Images:

- Raw Image and (dd format) – Bit-by-bit copy
- E01 Format – All the Compressed and supports metadata

Advantages of Disk Imaging:

- It Preserves all the original evidence
- And Allows repeated analysis
- To Captures deleted and hidden data

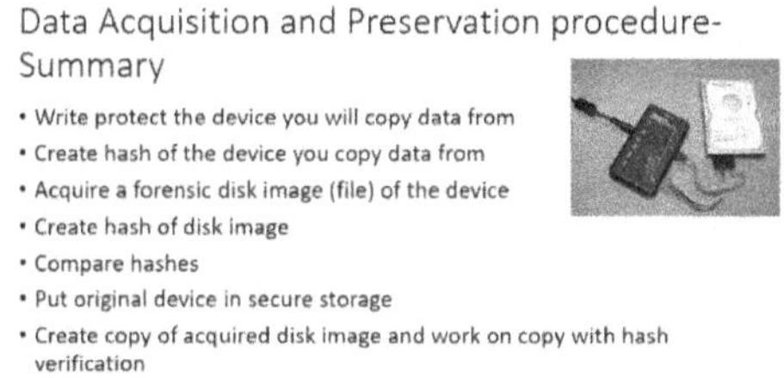

Figure 3.7: Data Acquisition and preservation using tools FTK imager and dc3dd

3.9 Hashing and Integrity Verification

Hashing is also plays and important role to ensure that evidence remains unchanged during acquisition and analysis.

A hash function is to generate a unique value for data. And Even a small change in the data results in a completely a different hash value. Hashing is very important in the field of forensics because the digital evidence must be verified at different stages of the investigation. By comparing the hash values before but after the acquisition or analysis, investigators can confirm that the data has not been tampered. And this can helps maintain the trust in the evidence.

Common hashing algorithms are used in forensic and works include MD5, SHA-1, and SHA-256. These are algorithms that convert data into a fixed-length value that can acts like a digital fingerprint of the file or storage media. If the content changes, the resulting hash and the value will also change.

Common Hash Algorithms:

- MD5
- SHA-1
- SHA-256

Verification Process:

1. Generate the hash of original device
2. Generate the hash of forensic image
3. Compare all the values

If it both match, then the integrity is confirmed.

3.10 Evidence Documentation and Reporting

Proper documentation is essential for maintaining transparency and ensuring that findings can be verified. In a simple terms, the documentation means the recording of every important step taken during the investigation in a clear and organized manner. It is also important because the forensic findings should be understandable, repeatable, and it should be open to review by other experts or legal authorities.

Good documentation may also include case details, date and time of actions, tools used, acquisition methods, hash values, observations, screenshots, recovered evidence, and the analyst notes. Each are every steps are recorded and should be accurate and written in a professional manner.

Reporting is the final stage where the technical findings should be presented in a clear form for investigators, management, or the court. For an example, a report may be explained how deleted files were recovered or it is how suspicious activity was identified on the device. Because of this, the proper documentation and reporting it strengthen the credibility of the entire forensic investigation.

Documentation Includes:

- The Case details
- The Evidence description
- All the Tools and techniques used
- Steps should be followed
- All the Observations and findings

A well-documented report will strengthens the credibility of the investigation.

3.11 Case Study: Evidence Handling in Insider Data Theft

A company is to suspects that an employee has copied confidential files and deleted them before leaving.

Investigation Steps:

1. The System identified and isolated
2. All the Evidence labeled and documented
3. Used Write blocker used to access disk
4. The Disk image created using FTK Imager
5. The Hash values generated and verified
6. The Chain of custody is maintained
7. And the Analysis performed on forensic image

Findings:

- The Files accessed late at night
- USB device connected
- Particular Files that is been deleted shortly after

Conclusion:

Proper evidence handling can be ensured that findings were:

- Are Accurate
- And can be Verifiable
- It's Legally admissible

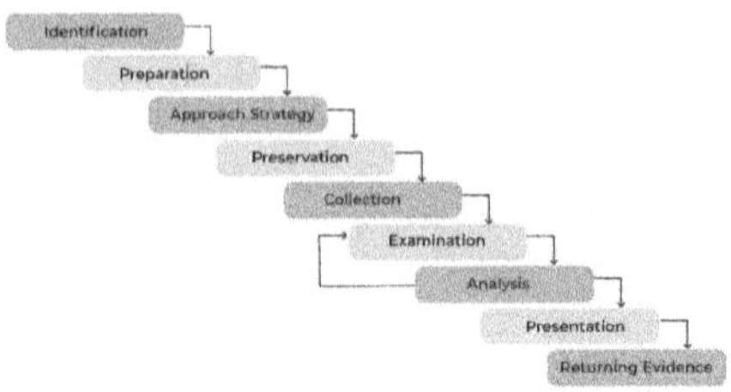

Figure 3.8: Case Investigation Workflow

3.12 Practical Lab: Evidence Handling and Imaging

Objective:

To understand how the digital evidence is handled and imaged.

Procedure:

1. To Identify evidence source
2. Should Use write blocker
3. Create the forensic image
4. Generate the hash values
5. Document all the steps

Expected Outcome:

- Evidence integrity are maintained
- Forensic image are created
- Proper documentation are being made

3.13 Key Points

- Digital evidence is the fragile and must be handled carefully
- Chain of custody ensures the accountability
- Disk imaging protects the original data
- Write blockers used to prevent modification
- Hashing verifies the integrity of the final extracted data

3.14 Summary

This chapter has given and overview and discussed the critical aspects of the evidence handling in digital forensics. It is emphasized the importance of preserving the evidence integrity, and maintaining chain of custody, and using proper acquisition techniques such as disk imaging and hashing.

By following these principles, the investigators can ensure that the digital evidence remains reliable and admissible in legal proceedings.

3.15 Review Questions

Short Answer:

1. What is chain of custody?
2. What is disk imaging?
3. Why are write blockers used?

Long Answer:

1. Explain the evidence handling lifecycle?
2. Discuss the importance of hashing in digital forensics?

3.16 Practical Exercise

A computer is suspected in a cybercrime case.

- Describe how you will handle the evidence?
- Explain how chain of custody will be maintained?
- Outline the imaging process?
- Describe how integrity will be verified?

Multiple Choice Questions

1. Digital evidence is:
   A. Stable
   B. Fragile
   C. Permanent
   D. Visible
   Answer: B
2. Integrity means:
   A. Data speed
   B. Data unchanged
   C. Data encrypted
   D. Data deleted
   Answer: B
3. Chain of custody tracks:
   A. Files
   B. Evidence handling
   C. Logs
   D. Network
   Answer: B
4. Write blocker prevents:
   A. Reading
   B. Writing
   C. Copying
   D. Deleting
   Answer: B
5. Disk imaging creates:
   A. Backup
   B. Exact copy
   C. Log
   D. Cache
   Answer: B
6. Hash mismatch indicates:
   A. Integrity maintained
   B. Data altered
   C. Data deleted
   D. Data compressed
   Answer: B
7. Evidence lifecycle includes:
   A. Identification
   B. Collection
   C. Analysis
   D. All
   Answer: D
8. Documentation ensures:
   A. Speed

B. Legal validity
C. Storage
D. Encryption
Answer: B

9. Authenticity confirms:
A. Data size
B. Source validity
C. Speed
D. Format
Answer: B

10. Evidence must be analyzed on:
A. Original device
B. Copy
C. RAM
D. Network
Answer: B

CHAPTER 4

File Systems and Data Acquisition in Digital Forensics

4.1 Introduction

In digital forensic of investigations, there is a visible interface of a computer system that represents only a fraction of the available evidence. Beneath that the graphical user will interface with the lies of a complex structure where data is being stored, organized, and it is managed. This are the structure that is known as the file system that plays a crucial role in determining how the information is written to and what is retrieved from storage devices.

Whenever a user are interacts with a system—it creates a file, editing a document, copying data, or deleting an information—these are the actions that are recorded in some form within the file system. Even attempts to conceal or to destroy the evidence it often leave behind traces that can be uncovered through a careful forensic analysis.

Equally it is important in the process of data acquisition, which involves the collecting digital evidence in such a manner that preserves its integrity. And Without proper acquisition techniques, the evidence may become tampered, corrupted, or it can be legally inadmissible.

This chapter also provides a detailed understanding of the file systems, storage structures, a deleted data, and the forensic acquisition techniques. It is a forms of the technical foundation that is required for conducting effective digital forensic investigations.

4.2 Concept and Function of File Systems

A file system is also a logical framework that can enables an operating system to store, organize, and manage the data on the storage devices such as hard disks, solid-state drives, and removable media.

It can performs very several critical functions:

- Have to organize the data into files and directories
- Have to Manage the storage space efficiently
- By Keeping track of file locations
- And Maintaining access permissions
- By Recording the timestamps related to file activity

Without a file system, the data would exist as an unstructured binary sequences, it can make extremely difficult to interpret or retrieve the meaningful information.

From a forensic standpoint, the file systems are very important because they are store not only the actual data (file content) but also the metadata, which can provides the contextual information about the user activity.

4.3 Role of File Systems in Digital Forensics

File systems act as a digital record of user interactions with a system. And even when the users attempt to hide their activities, the traces often remain in embedded within the file system.

Investigators are very much rely on file systems to:

- Identify it when files were created, accessed, or it is modified
- Detect the suspicious or all the unauthorized activities
- To recover deleted or hidden data
- To analyze the file relationships and structures
- Reconstruct sequences of the events (timeline analysis)

For instance, in a corporate data theft case, but the actual confidential file can may no longer be present on the very system. However, the file system and the metadata may still reveal that the file was existed, and it was accessed at a specific time, and was later been deleted.

Thus, the file systems provide the both direct evidence (file data) and indirect evidence (metadata and logs).

4.4 Types of File Systems

The different types of the file system operating systems use different file systems, each are with its own structure and characteristics. And a forensic investigator must be familiar with all these systems to interpret the evidence correctly. A file system is the method that used by an operating system to organize, store, retrieve, and also to manage the data on a storage device. It is very important because the way files are being arranged can be affected how the evidence is found and interpreted during the investigation. There are Different file systems store metadata, timestamps, permissions, and deleted data in different ways.

In the practice, the investigators are often examine the file system structures to understand that the user activity, recover deleted files, and trace the changes made to the system. For an example, a deleted document still may be recoverable from the one file system, while the file system may overwrite that space more quickly. And Because of this, the knowledge of file systems is very essential in digital forensics.

An Common examples of the file systems that can include FAT and NTFS used in the Windows systems, ext3/ext4 used in Linux environments, and APFS or HFS+ used in Apple devices. Each of these has its unique features that can be become relevant during forensic analysis.

4.4.1 FAT (File Allocation Table)

File Allocation Table is one of the earliest file systems are used still widely in portable storage devices are as USB drives and memory cards.

Characteristics:

- The simple structure
- The high compatibility across the systems
- All the Limited security features

Forensic Significance:

- Deleted file and the entries may remain in the directory structure
- Easy to analyze that is due to simplicity

4.4.2 NTFS (New Technology File System)

NTFS is also the standard file that the system is used in modern times the windows operating systems.

Features:

- It's supports the large files and volumes
- It will Provide file permissions and the encryption
- Will Maintain journaling for recovery

Forensic Importance:

- The Uses of the **Master File Table (MFT)** to store the file records
- It will retains detailed metadata
- All the Useful for reconstructing the file activity and timelines

4.4.3 ext File System (Linux)

Linux systems are uses file systems such as ext3 and ext4.

Features:

- It Uses inode-based structure
- To Supports journaling

Forensic Importance:

- To Stores metadata in inodes
- All the Useful in server and enterprise investigations

4.4.4 APFS / HFS+ (Apple Systems)

Apple devices are used file systems such as HFS+ and APFS.

Forensic Importance:

- To supports snapshots and encryption
- And Maintains detailed metadata
- All the Important in mobile and Mac-based investigations

4.5 Structure of Storage Devices

The Data on a storage device are organized in the hierarchical layers, and each serving with a specific purpose.

Key Components:

- Sector: The smallest addressable unit of the storage
- Cluster: A group of a sectors that is used to store the file data
- Partition: An logical division of a disk
- Volume: A formatted partition with the file system

Files are stored in the clusters, and the large files may be a split across and the multiple clusters, and this phenomenon is known as fragmentation. Understanding the structure of the storage devices it is important because the digital evidence are physically stored in these layers. Investigators must know that where data is located and how it can managed in a order to recover the files, and detect hidden information, and to interpret the storage activity correctly.

In an practice, when a file is saved, the operating system are assigns the clusters and records its location by the file system. If the file grows larger, it can be stored in different non-contiguous clusters. This are fragmented storage and can make forensic recovery even more complex, especially when in some parts of the file have been deleted or overwritten.

Another the Important point is that the storage devices may be contain unallocated space, slack space, and hidden partitions. So these areas are sometimes store in the remnants of old data or deleted files that are not visible to normal users. For an example, the fragments of documents or images may still remain in the unused sectors and then it can be recovered during forensic investigation. Because of this, the knowledge of storage structure is very essential for accurate digital investigations.

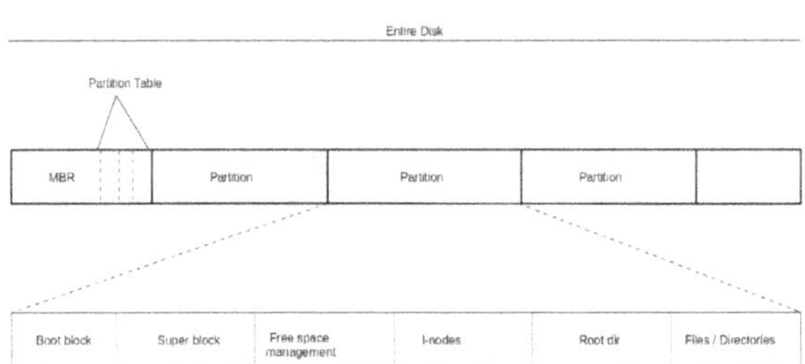

Fig 4.1: Structure of Disk Partitions and File System Layout

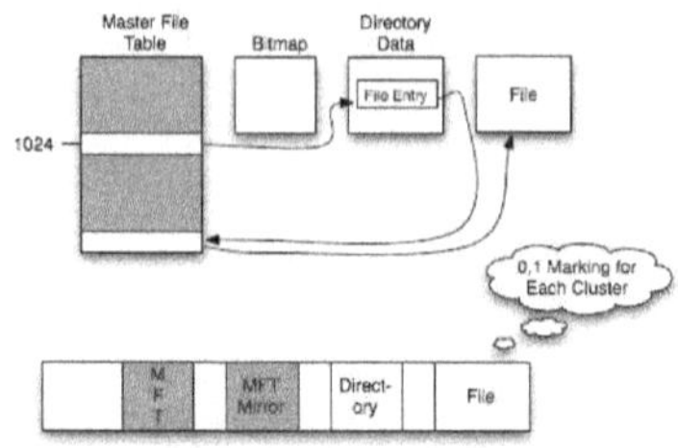

Fig 4.2: NTFS File System Architecture Showing Master File Table (MFT) Structure

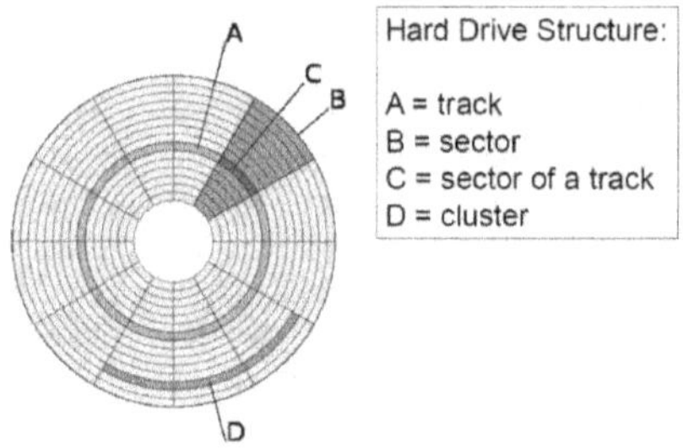

Fig 4.3: Physical Structure of Hard Disk Showing Tracks, Sectors, and Clusters

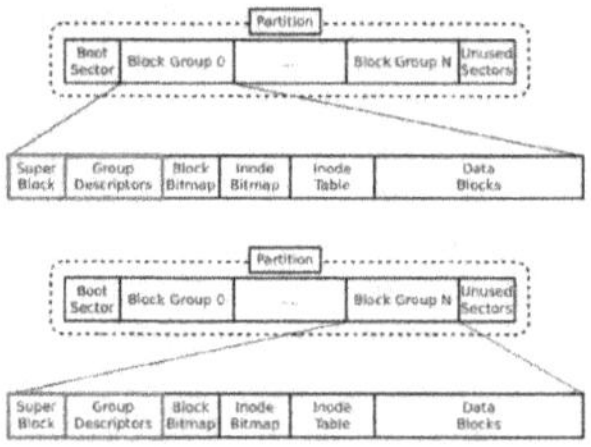

Fig 4.4: Structure of Linux File System Showing Superblock, Inodes, and Data Blocks

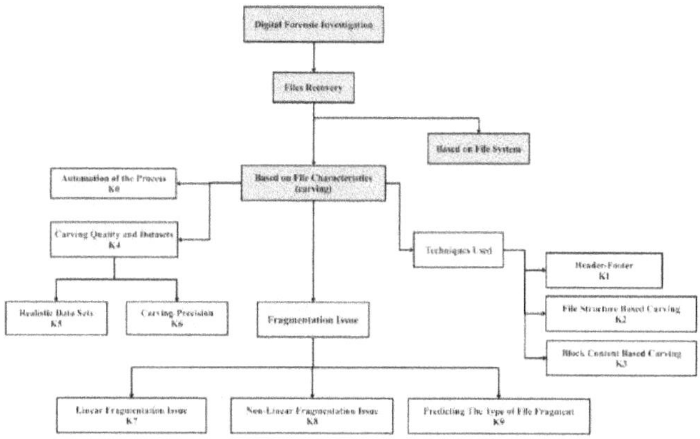

Fig 4.5: Data Recovery Process and File Carving Techniques in Digital Forensics

Explanation:

This are the figure that help us to illustrate how the data is structured within a storage device, and showing the partitions, clusters, and the file allocation areas.

4.6 Metadata and Its Forensic Value

Metadata are to refer the descriptive information about a file rather than its actual content. It provides a critical insights into file usage and the system activity. In a simple terms, the metadata is data about data. And it does not contain the main content of the file, but it can describes the important details that are related to that file. This is very valuable in digital forensics because the metadata can help examiner to understand when a file was created, accessed, modified, moved, or shared.

Common examples are of the metadata that include file name, file size, creation date, modification time, owner details, file path, permissions, and device information. In some of cases, documents and images may also can be store author names, software version, GPS coordinates, or camera details.

In a practice, the investigators used metadata to reconstruct it timelines and identify the user activity. For an example, if a document was not modified and shortly before an incident, that information can may become relevant to the case. And similarly, the photo metadata showing location in details may help its place or a person at a specific area. Because of this, the metadata often provides a strong supporting evidence during the forensic analysis.

Common Metadata Attributes:

- The File name
- It's File size
- It's Creation time
- The Last modified time
- Last accessed time
- The File path

Metadata is an extremely valuable in the field of forensic investigations because it allows the investigators to reconstruct the user behavior and even when the file content is missing.

For an example, the metadata can be reveal that a file was accessed at an unusual time or modified within shortly before deletion.

4.7 Deleted Files and Unallocated Space

When a file is deleted, it's operating system typically removes all its reference from the file system but it does not immediately erase all the actual data.

Instead:

- The space is occupied by the file is marked as an available
- The data still remains until it's overwritten

This unused space is known as unallocated space.

From a forensic perspective, the unallocated space are the highly valuable because it may contain:

- The Deleted files
- The Fragments of previous data
- All the Hidden artifacts

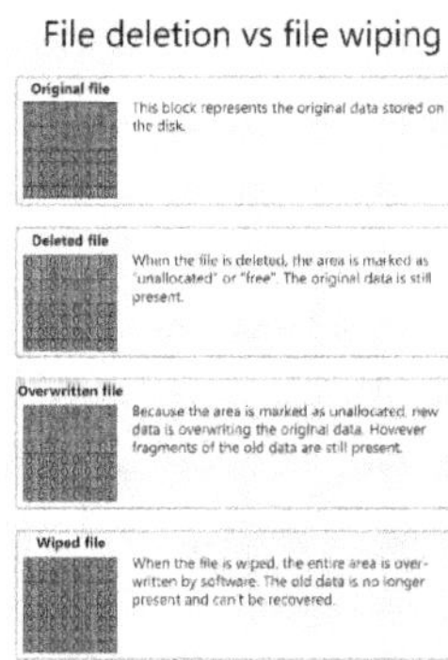

Figure 4.6: Deleted File Recovery Concept

Fig 4.7: Comparison of File Deletion Mechanisms in HDD and SSD with Forensic Implications

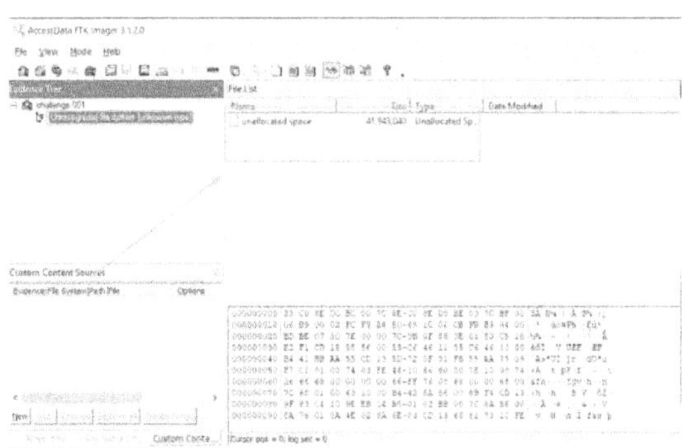

Fig 4.8: Analysis of Unrecognized File System Using FTK Imager and Hex View

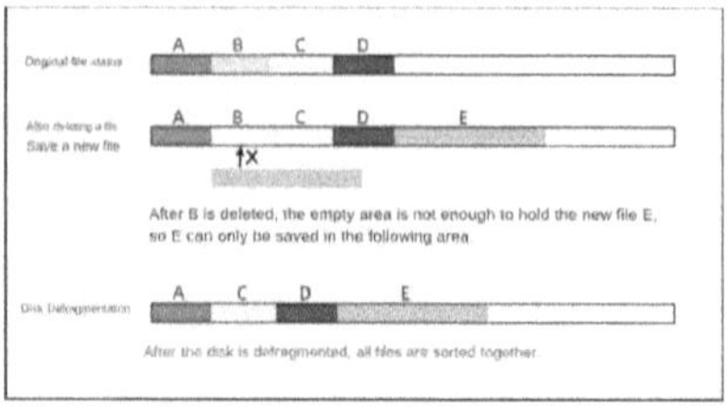

Fig 4.9: File Fragmentation and Defragmentation Process in Disk Storage

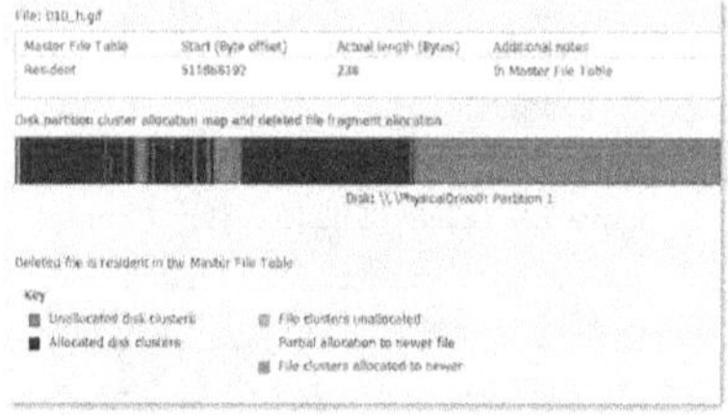

Fig 4.10: Cluster Allocation Map Showing Deleted File Fragments in NTFS

4.8 Data Acquisition in Digital Forensics

Data acquisition is the process of collecting the digital evidence in such a manner that ensures it remains unaltered and it is admissible in the court.

The primary objective is to create an exact duplicate of the original storage with the medium so that the analysis can be conducted without any modifying the original data. Data acquisition is considered it one of the most sensitive stages in a forensic investigation because of the quality to later analysis how it depends on how accurately the evidence is collected and in the beginning how it was collected. If any mistakes happen during this step, the important data may be lost or its authenticity may be questioned later in court.

In many cases, the investigators also uses forensic imaging tools all together with the write blockers to prevent any kind of accidental changes to the storage media in during acquisition. This helps in maintaining the integrity of the evidence throughout the investigation process.

For example, if a hard disk is seized from a suspect's computer, that the investigators will first create a forensic image of the drive and then he will perform the examination on the copied image instead of the original disk. Because of this, the original evidence will remain preserved for future verification or in the court presentation.

4.9 Importance of Data Acquisition

Proper data acquisition is very essential because:

- It will preserves the original evidence
- It will allows repeatable analysis
- It will ensures legal admissibility
- It will captures hidden and deleted data

Failure to follow any proper acquisition the procedures may result in loss of evidence or rejection in court. The importance of the data acquisition can also be understood with the fact that digital evidence is fragile in nature. And Even a small action in such as opening a file, connecting a device, or starting a system may can change timestamps or the system data. Because of this, the evidence must be collected very carefully and according to all standard procedures.

Another important point is that proper acquisition allows different experts to examine the same copied evidence again whenever required. This is very useful when the findings need verification, peer review, or presentation in court proceedings.

For an example, a deleted file can be recovered from a forensic image that can be rechecked later by another investigator without touching the original storage device. This will improves the reliability and credibility of the investigation.

4.10 The Types of Data Acquisition

4.10.1 Physical Acquisition

- It Creates a bit-by-bit copy of the entire disk
- It will Includes deleted files and unallocated space
- And Most comprehensive method

4.10.2 Logical Acquisition

- All the Copies only visible files
- And Faster but limited

4.10.3 Live Acquisition

- Should be Performed on a running system
- And Captures volatile data such as RAM

4.10.4 The Dead Acquisition

- Should Performed when system is powered off
- It is Safer for disk analysis

Fig 4.11: Comparison Between Live Forensics and Dead Forensics Investigation Approaches

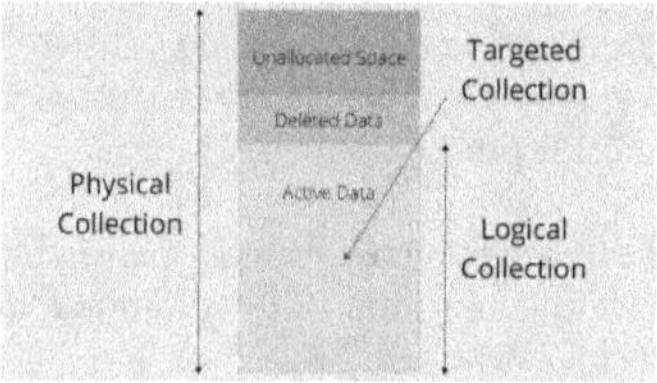

Fig 4.12: Comparison of Physical, Logical, and Targeted Data Collection Methods

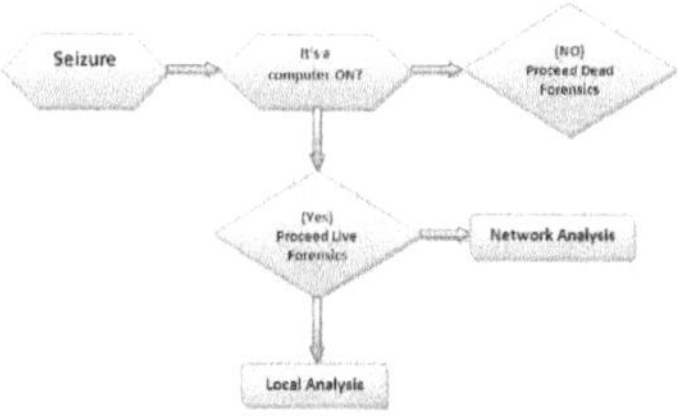

Fig 4.13: Decision-Making Workflow for Live and Dead Forensic Investigation

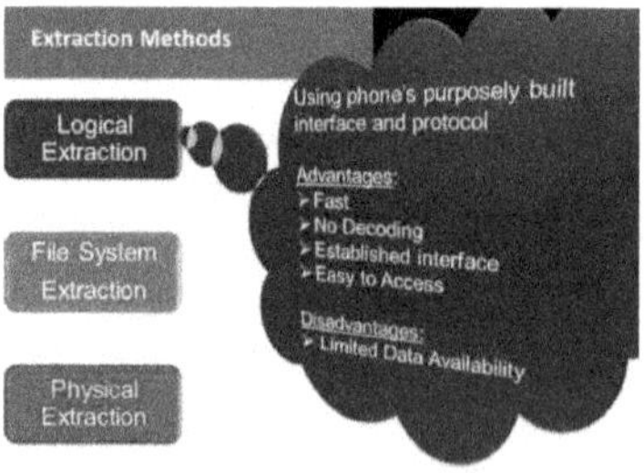

Fig 4.14: Mobile Data Extraction Methods in Digital Forensics

4.11 Forensic Imaging

Forensic imaging are involved in creating an exact replica of a storage device.

Tools such as:

- FTK Imager

are widely used to perform this process.

The resulting of the image contains:

- All active files
- All deleted data
- And file system structures

Forensic imaging is very important because it will allow investigators to examine the digital evidence without any directly working on the original device. In a simple terms, the image file can acts as a complete copy that can be later analyzed many times while the original media remains preserved and untouched.

In many cases in the field, forensic images can be verified by using hash values such as MD5 or SHA algorithms. If the hash value of the original device didn't match the hash value of the created image, it will proof that the copy is not accurate and changed. This step helps maintain evidence integrity.

For an example, when a investigator seized a laptop or hard drive is imaged using FTK Imager, the investigator can recover the deleted files, inspect folder structures, and search for the suspicious documents from the image file itself. Because of this, forensic imaging is a standard practice in the field of digital forensic investigations.

4.12 Hashing and Integrity Verification

Hashing is also used to verify that the acquired data is the identical to the original.

Common Algorithms are:

- MD5
- SHA-1
- SHA-256

If hash values match, it can confirms data integrity.

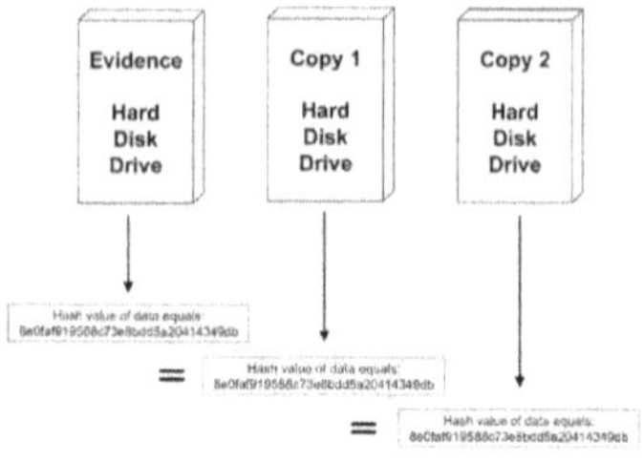

Figure 4.15: Hash Verification Process

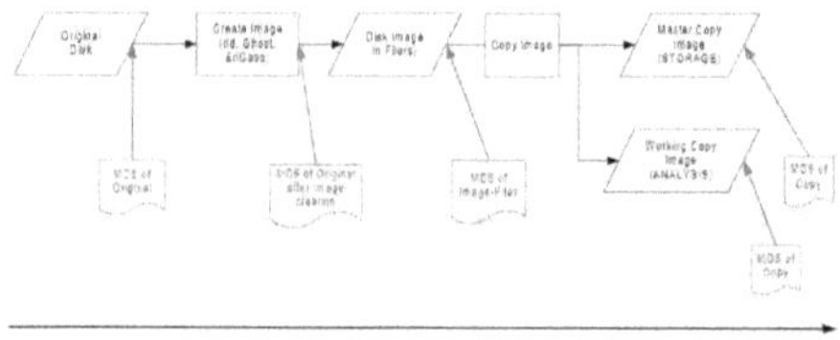

Fig 4.16: Digital Forensic Imaging Process with Hash Verification (MD5 Integrity Check)

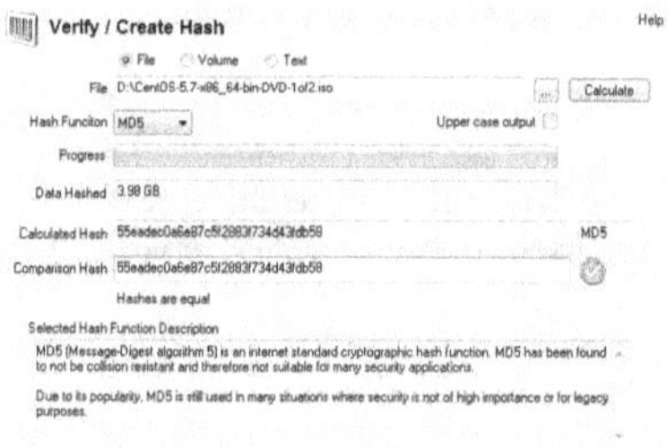

Fig 4.17: Workflow of Disk Imaging and Hash-Based Integrity Verification in Digital Forensics

4.13 Case Study: Forensic Recovery of Deleted Data

A computer system is too suspected of being used to copy the confidential academic of a project files. After copying the files, the user is to deletes them to avoid detection.

Investigation Approach:

- To Create forensic image
- To Analyze deleted files
- To Examine file metadata
- To Check external device activity

Findings:

- Files accessed at unusual time
- USB device connected
- Files deleted shortly after

Conclusion:

Digital evidence will confirms unauthorized copying and deletion of files.

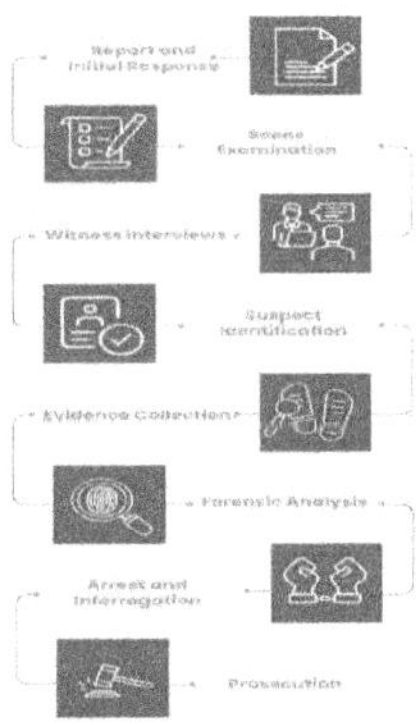

Figure 4.18: Timeline Reconstruction

Objective:

To perform a forensic imaging and recover deleted files.

Tools:

- FTK Imager
- Autopsy Digital Forensics Platform

Steps:

1. To Create disk image
2. To Generate hash
3. To Load image into analysis tool
4. And Recover deleted files
5. To Analyze metadata

4.15 Key Points

- File systems is to organize and manage data
- Metadata can provides us valuable forensic evidence
- The Deleted files can often be recovered
- Data acquisition also preserves evidence integrity
- Hashing ensures the authenticity

4.16 Summary

This chapter is explored the structure and importance of file systems and it is explained how the digital evidence is acquired in a forensic investigations. Understanding the storage mechanisms and acquisition the techniques enables investigators to recover the hidden data and reconstruct events effectively.

4.17 Review Questions

Short:

1. What is a file system?
2. Define what is metadata?
3. What is unallocated space?

Long:

1. Explain the file system types
2. Discuss data acquisition methods

4.18 Practical Exercise

A system shows a signs of unauthorized file access and deletion.

- Identify evidence sources
- Suggest the acquisition method
- Explain how a integrity will be verified

Multiple Choice Questions

1. File system manages:
   A. Hardware
   B. Data storage
   C. Network
   D. BIOS
   Answer: B
2. FAT is:
   A. Modern secure FS
   B. Old file system
   C. Cloud system
   D. RAM system
   Answer: B
3. NTFS uses:
   A. FAT table
   B. MFT
   C. RAM
   D. BIOS
   Answer: B
4. Metadata includes:
   A. File content
   B. Timestamps
   C. Images
   D. Programs
   Answer: B
5. Deleted files remain in:
   A. RAM
   B. Unallocated space
   C. BIOS
   D. Cache
   Answer: B
6. Physical acquisition captures:
   A. Partial data
   B. Full disk
   C. Only files
   D. Only logs
   Answer: B
7. Logical acquisition captures:
   A. Entire disk
   B. Visible data
   C. RAM
   D. Logs
   Answer: B
8. Hashing ensures:
   A. Speed

B. Integrity
C. Storage
D. Encryption
Answer: B

9. Cluster is:
A. Smallest unit
B. Group of sectors
C. File
D. Program
Answer: B

10. Fragmentation means:
A. Data deleted
B. Data split
C. Data encrypted
D. Data copied
Answer: B

CHAPTER 5

Digital Forensic Tools and Practical Analysis

5.1 Introduction

In the field of Cyber forensics the Digital forensic investigations are not limited to the theoretical understanding but also they require the effective and should be used of specialized tools to collect, analyze, and interpret the digital evidence. In the modern environments, the volume of digital data is very large, and making it manual the analysis are inefficient and often impractical.

Forensic tools are designed to assist the investigators in:

- Extracting relevant of data from storage devices
- To Recovering deleted or hidden files
- And Analyzing system and application logs
- To Monitoring and interpreting network traffic

These tools can follow the standardized forensic methodologies to ensure that the evidence remains reliable and it is admissible in legal proceedings.

This chapter also provides a detailed overview of the commonly used digital forensic tools and explains how they are applied in the real-world investigations through an structured workflows and practical examples.

5.2 Role and Importance of Forensic Tools

The complexity of modern digital the systems can make the forensic tools essential. Investigators must deal with large volumes of data and unstructured data, often it spread across multiple devices and platforms in the field of forensics.

Forensic tools can help in:

- Automation of repetitive tasks such as the file indexing and keyword searching
- Efficient data processing is to handle large datasets
- Also the Accurate recovery of deleted data
- Visualization of the timelines and relationships
- Maintaining the integrity through controlled processes

Without these tools, the investigations it would be more time-consuming, error-prone, and difficult to validate.

5.3 Categories of Digital Forensic Tools

Forensic tools can be classified and it is based on their primary function and there are different forensic investigations that require different types of tools. Not a single tool is very enough for every situation, so every tools are usually in grouped according to the task and how they perform. This will help the investigators to choose the most suitable software or hardware for a specific case.

Common categories are been include for acquisition tools, analysis tools, recovery tools, network forensic tools, mobile forensic tools, and memory analysis tools, for reporting tools. Each and every category is to designed and to solve a particular problem during the investigation process are given below:

1. Acquisition Tools

It is used for collecting data without altering the original evidence.

For Example:

- FTK Imager

2. Analysis Tools

For the examining data it is used and extracting meaningful information.

For Example:

- The Autopsy Digital Forensics Platform

3. Network Forensic Tools

It is used to capture and analyze network traffic.

For Example:

- Wireshark

4. Mobile and Specialized Tools

Used for the mobile devices, the memory analysis, and advanced investigations.

5.4 Disk Imaging Using FTK Imager

FTK Imager

FTK Imager are used very widely and used to acquisition tool that allows the investigators to create exact copies of the storage devices and while maintaining data integrity.

Key Features:

- Bit-by-bit imaging
- Help in Supports multiple formats (RAW, E01)
- To Generates hash values
- And Allows preview of files

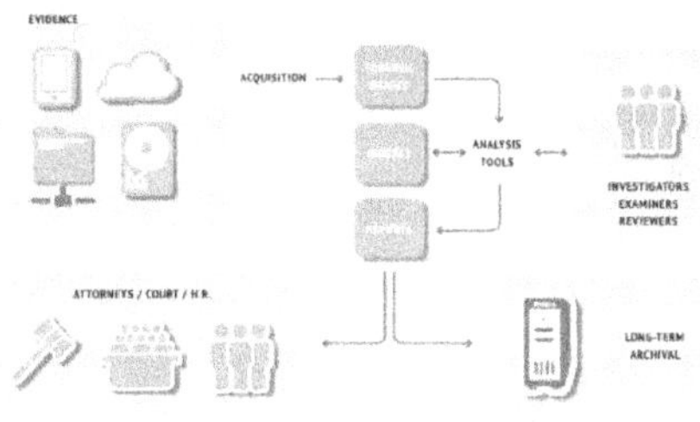

Figure 5.1: Disk Imaging Workflow

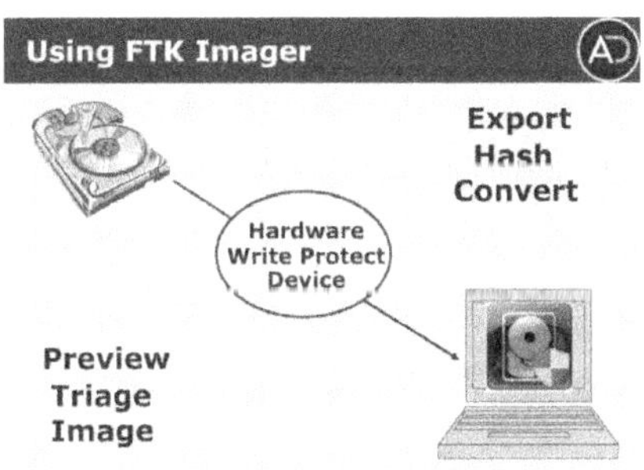

Fig 5.2: FTK Imager Workflow with Hardware Write Protection

Detailed Procedure:

1. To Launch FTK Imager
2. And Select the "Create Disk Image"
3. To Choose source type (physical/logical drive)
4. To Select evidence source
5. Choose the image destination
6. Enable the hash calculation
7. Start the imaging process

Forensic Insight:

Imaging ensures that:

- The original data evidence is not modified
- Deleted and hidden data are to be preserved
- Analysis can be repeated multiple times

5.5 Disk Analysis Using Autopsy

Autopsy Digital Forensics Platform

Autopsy is an open-source in the field of forensic platform that is used to analyze disk images and recover the digital evidence. Autopsy is also used widely and used in the academic and its professional environments because it can provide a user-friendly and interface for examining the digital evidence. It will help the investigators to analyze file systems, recover deleted files, search keywords, and to review the user activity from forensic images.

In a practice, the examiner loads a disk image into Autopsy and then the tool automatically processes the important artifacts such as web history, emails, documents, installed programs, and timeline data. This can saves time and help the organize in a large amounts of evidence.

Key Features:

- The File system analysis
- And Recover the Deleted file
- Keyword search
- Timeline and generation
- And to create report

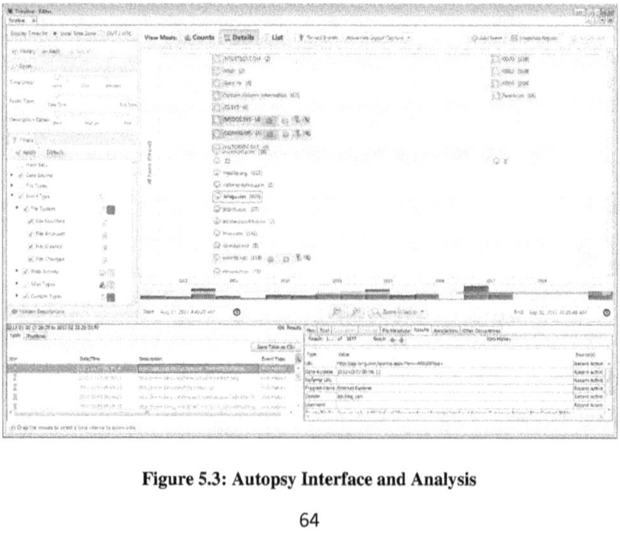

Figure 5.3: Autopsy Interface and Analysis

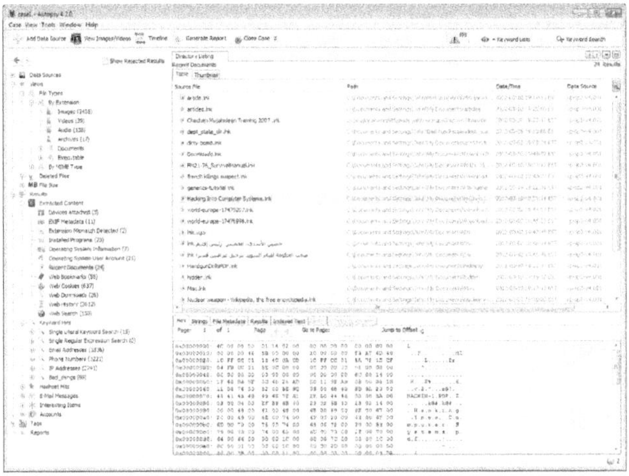

Fig 5.4: Access the Data FTK (Forensic Toolkit) Interface

Detailed the Workflow:

1. To Create a new case
2. Add the disk image
3. Select the ingest modules
4. Perform the analysis
5. Review results:
   - Deleted files
   - File metadata
   - Timeline

Forensic Insight:

Autopsy are converts into raw data:

- The readable information
- And structured the evidence
- To visual timelines

5.6 Network Analysis Using Wireshark

Wireshark

Wireshark is also used to capture and analyze the network traffic in real time. With it the Wireshark is one of the most popular and commonly used tools for network forensics because it allows the investigators to inspect the packets from moving across a network in the real time. It will help to identify the suspicious and for communication, protocol misuse, connection attempts, and unusual traffic patterns.

In a practice, The Wireshark are to captures packets and displays the detailed information such as source IP address, destination IP address, protocol type, ports, timestamps, and packet contents. It also provides the filters that will make it easier to focus on the specific traffic during analysis.

Key Features:

- The Packet capture
- Protocol the analysis
- Filtering the capabilities
- Should Traffic inspection

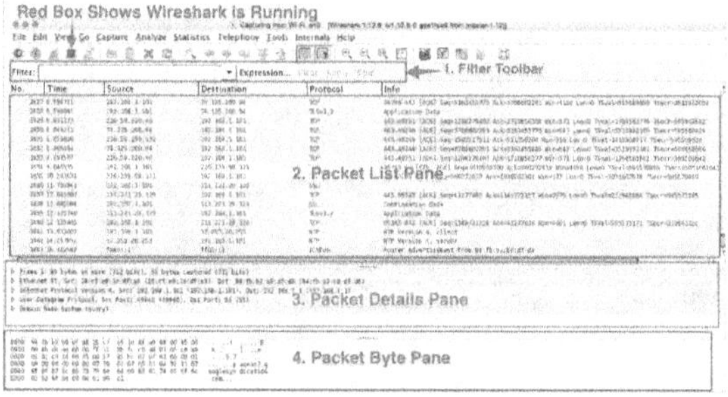

Figure 5.5: Packet Analysis in Wireshark

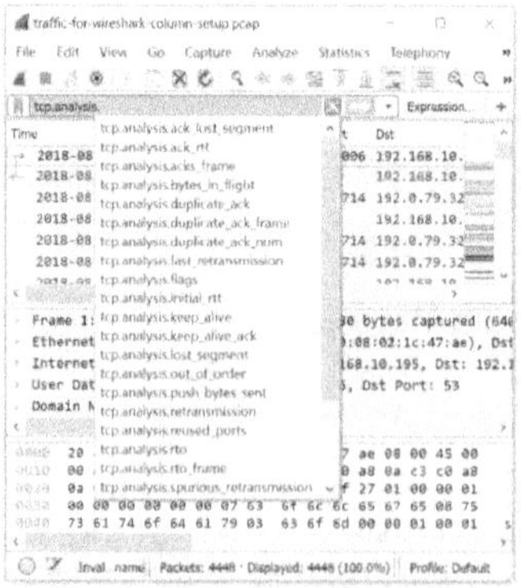

Fig 5.6: Wireshark TCP Analysis Filter Options Interface

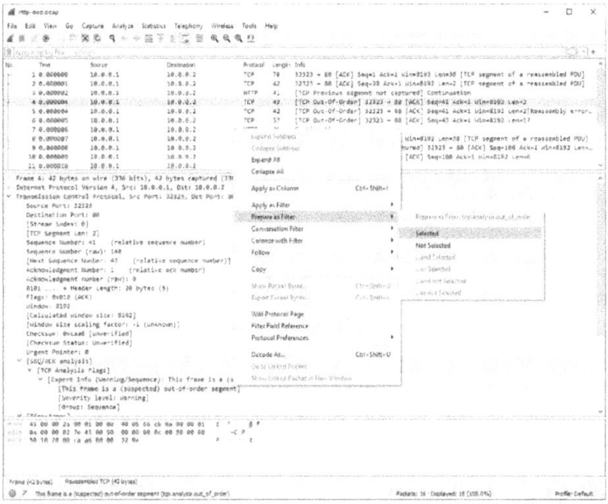

Fig 5.7: Wireshark Packet Analysis with TCP Out-of-Order Detection

Procedure:

1. To Start the packet capture
2. And Apply filters (e.g., HTTP, DNS)
3. To Analyze packet details
4. Identify suspicious patterns

Forensic Insight:

Network analysis are useful to help identifying:

- To unauthorized connections
- And data exfiltration
- malware communication

5.7 Keyword Search and Data Filtering

Digital forensic uses tools that allow to search through the large datasets using the keywords. Keyword and search the data filtering are very important because of the modern devices and may contains thousands or even millions of the files. Manually the checking of each file and it would take a lot of time, so that the investigators uses an search functions to quickly locate relevant information.

In the practice, forensic tools are allowed to search based on the words, file names, email addresses, dates, extensions, metadata, and it content patterns. The Filters can also be applied to narrow the results by the file type, user activity, time period, or specific folders. This will makes the investigation more focused and efficient.

For Example:

- Email IDs
- Passwords
- File names

This are the technique that helps the investigators quickly to locate relevant evidence within massive data volumes.

5.8 Timeline Analysis

To timeline the analysis is one of the most powerful features of forensic tools. That helps to reconstruct events in chronological order. Timeline and analysis are very important because it helps the investigators to arrange the digital events in an order they occurred. By viewing the activities chronologically, it will becomes easier to understand the user actions, identify suspicious behavior, and to connect different pieces of evidence.

In the practice, a forensic tools collect all the timestamps from the files, logs, browser history, emails, application records, and system events. These are the timestamps should be organized into a timeline that shows what will happened before, during, and after an incident. This will provides a clearer picture of the case.

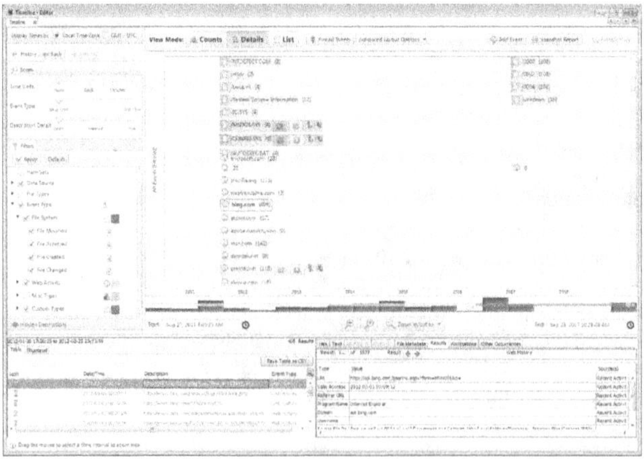

Fig 5.8: Autopsy Timeline Analysis View (Digital Forensics Timeline Reconstruction)

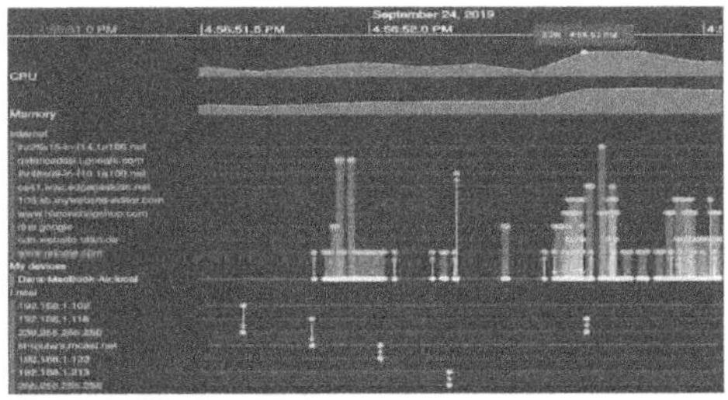

Fig 5.9: Network Traffic Visualization Dashboard (Packet/Traffic Analysis Graph)

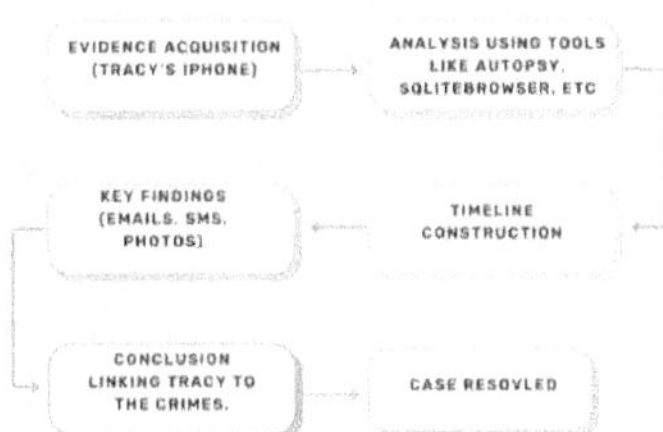

Fig 5.10: Digital Forensic Investigation Process Flowchart

The Data Sources for Timeline:

- File metadata
- System logs
- Application logs

Forensic Insight:

Timeline helps answer:

- What happened first?
- What actions followed?
- When did the incident occur?

5.9 Integrated Case Study: Tool-Based Investigation

Scenario:

A system is been suspected of unauthorized data transfer.

Investigation Steps:

Step 1: Imaging
Using FTK Imager
→ Create a disk image

Step 2: Analysis
Using Autopsy Digital Forensics Platform
→ Recover the deleted files
→ Analyze the metadata

Step 3: Network Investigation
Using the Wireshark
→ Identify the suspicious traffic

Findings:

- The Files is accessed at unusual time
- To Data transferred externally
- And Suspicious IP communication

Conclusion:

Combined use of tools are enabled to complete the reconstruction of the incident.

Figure 5.11: Tool-Based Investigation Workflow

5.10 Practical Lab: Complete Forensic Investigation

Objective:

Perform a full forensic to investigation the using tools.

Procedure:

1. To Acquire disk image
2. And Verify hash
3. Analyze using Autopsy
4. Recover the deleted files
5. Perform the keyword search
6. Generate the timeline
7. Analyze network data (optional)

Expected Results:

- The Evidence identified
- Deleted files are recovered
- Timeline are constructed
- Incident are understood

5.11 Advantages and Limitations of Forensic Tools

Advantages:

- To Faster analysis
- And Accurate results
- Handles the large datasets

Limitations:

- To Requires expertise
- Tool are dependency
- Possible false positives

5.12 Key Points

- Forensic tools are very essential for investigation
- Imaging tools is for preserve the evidence
- Analysis tools to extract insights
- Network tools is for detecting the communication
- Practical usage is critical

5.13 Summary

This chapter has provided a comprehensive understanding of the digital forensic tools and their practical applications. It has demonstrated how the tools are used to acquire, analyze, and interpret the digital evidence. By combining the multiple tools, the investigators can reconstruct incidents and uncover the hidden information.

5.14 Review Questions

Short:

1. What is FTK Imager used for?
2. What is Autopsy?
3. What is Wireshark?

Long:

1. Explain classification of forensic tools?
2. Describe tool-based investigation workflow?

5.15 Practical Exercise

A system shows suspicious activity.

- Select appropriate tools ?
- Describe investigation steps?
- Explain expected findings?

Multiple Choice Questions

1. Forensic tools help in:
   A. Deleting data
   B. Analysis
   C. Hiding logs
   D. Encrypting files
   Answer: B
2. FTK Imager is used for:
   A. Analysis
   B. Imaging
   C. Networking
   D. Reporting
   Answer: B
3. Autopsy is:
   A. Imaging tool
   B. Analysis tool
   C. Network tool
   D. Encryption tool
   Answer: B
4. Wireshark analyzes:
   A. Files
   B. Packets
   C. RAM
   D. Logs
   Answer: B
5. Keyword search helps:
   A. Delete data
   B. Find relevant info
   C. Encrypt files
   D. Compress data
   Answer: B
6. Timeline analysis shows:
   A. File size
   B. Sequence of events
   C. Passwords
   D. IP only
   Answer: B
7. Acquisition tools:
   A. Analyze data
   B. Collect data
   C. Encrypt data
   D. Delete data
   Answer: B

8. Analysis tools:
   A. Collect data
   B. Examine data
   C. Delete data
   D. Store data
   Answer: B
9. Network tools detect:
   A. File changes
   B. Communication
   C. RAM usage
   D. BIOS
   Answer: B
10. Limitation of tools:
   A. Fast
   B. Requires expertise
   C. Accurate
   D. Automated
   Answer: B

CHAPTER 6

Network and Mobile Forensics

6.1 Introduction

With the rapid growth of the mobile technologies and the internet usage, the cybercrimes are no longer only limited to the standalone computer systems. Today, as many as attacks are involved with the network communication and mobile devices. Because of this, the network and due to this mobile forensics have become an important part of digital investigations. The Network forensics is mainly about capturing, recording, and analyzing the network traffic to detect a suspicious activities or malicious activities. It can becomes useful because the many attackers leaves no traces while communicating through the networks. These traces can appear in the packets, logs, or unusual connections between the systems. As we can see In many cases, the investigators use this information to understand how the attack has happened. But, nowadays, people often use their mobile devices for almost everything - from talking to friends and family, to the banking and social media, to storing all their personal stuff. That's why the mobile forensics is so much important. It's all about getting and examining the data from smartphones, tablets, and other portable devices. These are the devices that can hold a lot of useful evidence, like messages, call logs, emails, photos, browsing history, and even where you've been through location tracker. For an instance, even if you've deleted a chat on the WhatsApp or your GPS history, still it can be found and used to figure out if you were their or involved in something. This are the kind of evidence and can be really helpful in the investigations. Mobile devices are like little treasure that stores a troves of information, and the mobile forensics is the key to unlocking it all. By looking at the data on these devices, the investigators can gather pieces together what have happened, and even if the investigator to find clues that might have been missed otherwise. So, that whether it's a crime scene or just a mystery, the mobile forensics can help all together to get into the bottom of things. There are also challenges In both the areas, though challenges. For one, there's a huge amount of data from the mobile phones that needs to be looked at. There is a problem of encryption and the device security, which can make it hard to get access. And it can make the matters worse, some of the information is only available for a short period of time, so if you don't collect it quickly, it might be loose for good.

PART A: NETWORK FORENSICS

6.2 Concept of Network Forensics

Network forensics is also a process of monitoring, capturing, and analyzing the network traffic to investigate the cyber incidents. In a simple terms, the network forensics are focuses on the examining communication of the data that will travels across the network such as the internet, local networks, or wireless environments. It is an important because many of the cyberattacks depend on the network connections to spread malware, steal data, or gain unauthorized access.

In a practice, the investigators collect the packet captures, firewall logs, router logs, intrusion detection alerts, and the server records to understand all the suspicious activity. By analyzing this information, it can be traced by the communication paths, identify attacker systems, and determine how the incident can be occurred.

It will help to answer the questions such as:

- What was the data transmitted?
- Who has been communicating with whom?
- When the communication did occur?
- Was the activity malicious?

Unlike the disk forensics, the network forensics are being dealing with the real-time and transient data, making it timely for collection and critical.

6.3 Types of Network Data

Network evidence also can be obtained from the multiple sources:

- From Packet captures (PCAP files)
- Firewall logs
- Router logs
- Server logs
- Intrusion detection systems

Each source will provides us a different perspective of network activity.

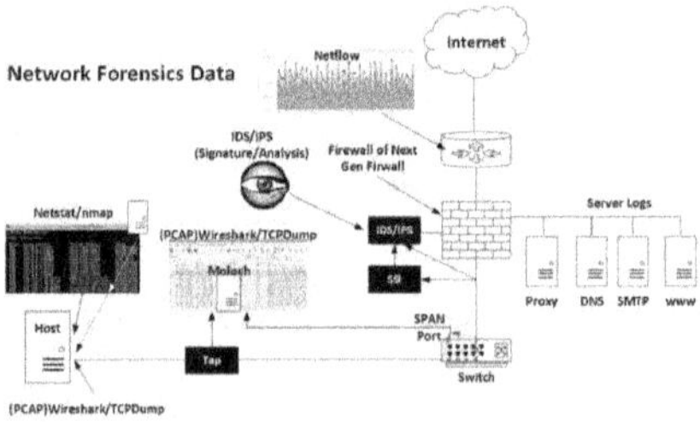

Figure 6.1: Network Forensics Data Sources

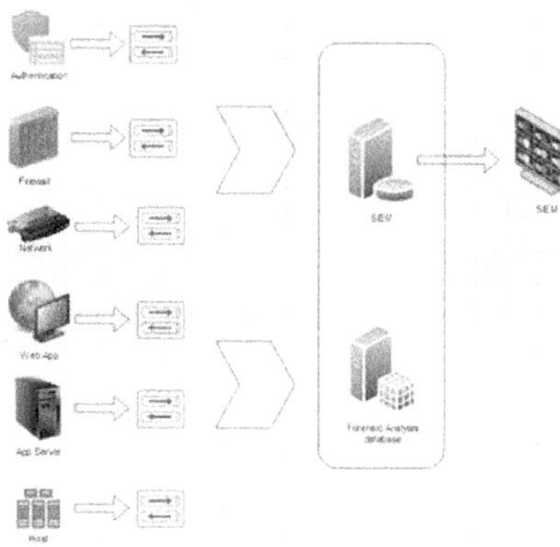

Fig 6.2: Security Information and Event Management (SIEM) Architecture for Digital Forensics

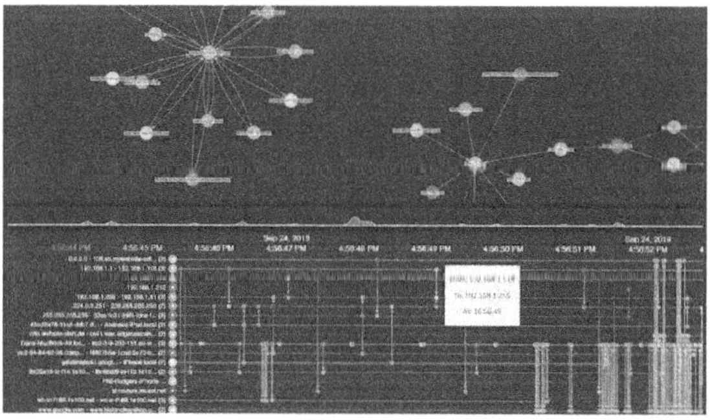

Fig 6.3: Network Traffic Correlation and Visualization Graph

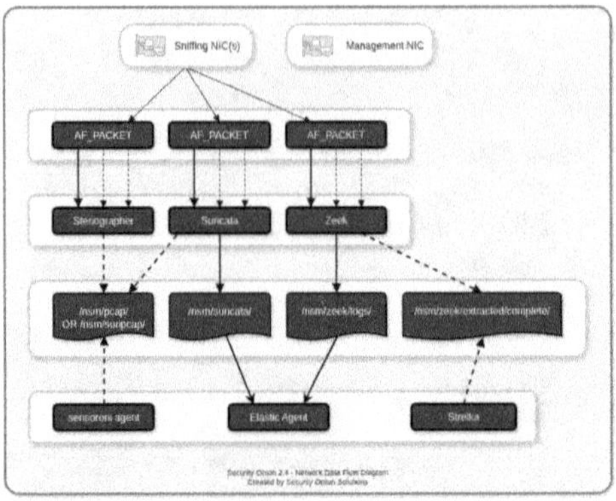

Fig 6.4: Security Onion Network Monitoring Data Flow Diagram

6.4 Packet Capture and Analysis

Packet capture are involved with the recording of the network traffic for analysis. Packet are captured and then it is been analysis and it is important because the network communication is divided into small units called packets. Each of the packet may contain very useful details such as source address, destination address, protocol type, timestamps, and the transmitted data. By examining these packets, the investigators can understand what has happened on the network.

In a practice, tools such as Wireshark are used to capture the traffic and to inspect packet contents. Investigators can also apply filters to focus on the specific IP addresses, ports, or protocols. This will helps to reduce large amounts of traffic and makes the suspicious activity easier to identify.

Tool Like:

- Wireshark

Key Concepts are:

- Packet: smallest unit of the network data
- Protocol: communication rules (TCP, UDP, HTTP)
- Header: That contains source/destination info

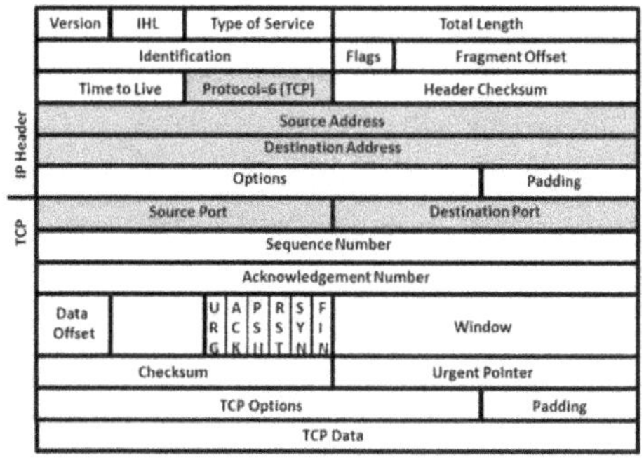

Figure 6.5: Packet Structure

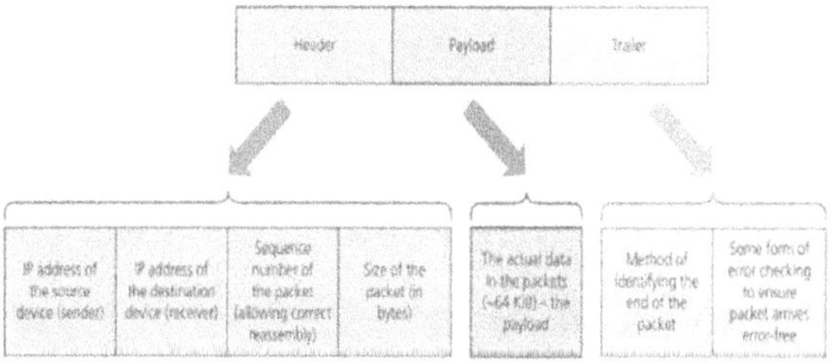

Fig 6.6: Network Packet Structure (Header, Payload, Trailer)

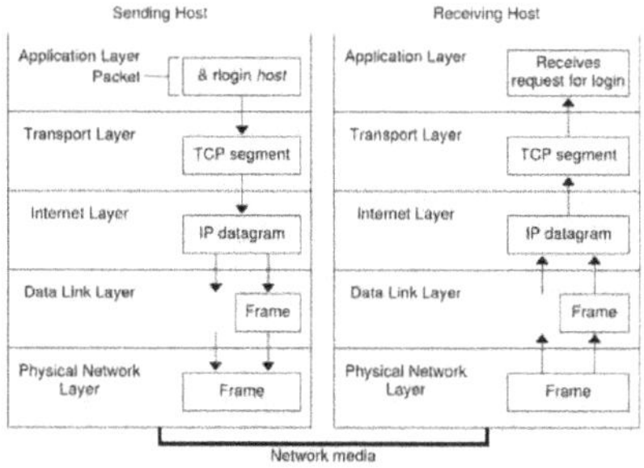

Fig 6.7: TCP/IP Encapsulation and DE capsulation Process

Steps in Packet Analysis:

1. To Capture the network traffic
2. To Apply the filters (IP, protocol)

3. And Analyze the packet details
4. Identify suspicious behavior

6.5 Network Forensic Techniques

1. Traffic Analysis are:

- To Observe the communication patterns
- And to Identifying unusual traffic

2. Log Analysis are:

- For Reviewing system and network logs
- And Identifying anomalies

3. Session Reconstruction are:

- To Rebuilding the communication sessions
- Understanding the attacker behavior

4. Intrusion Detection are:

- Detecting unauthorized access

6.6 Indicators of Network Attacks

- The Unusual traffic spikes
- And Unknown IP connections
- Repeated login attempts
- Data transfer to external servers

These are indicators that is important because of the abnormal network behavior are often provides in the early signs of a malicious activity. Investigators uses such a warning signs to detect the attacks, begin analysis, and then reduce any further damage to systems or data. A single indicator may not always confirm that an attack, but a multiple indicators can together become a highly suspicious.

In a practice, the unusual traffic spikes may get suggest the denial-of-service activity or a large unauthorized downloads. Any Unknown IP connections can indicate the communication with suspicious of external systems. Repeated login attempts can may be linked to a brute-force attacks, while an unexpected data transfers to the outside and servers can suggest the data theft or exfiltration.

6.7 Case Study: Network Intrusion Investigation

Scenario:

A company that have detected an unusual outbound the traffic from its server.

Investigation:

- To Capture traffic using Wireshark
- And Analyze suspicious IP addresses
- To Identify data transfer patterns

Findings:

- The Unauthorized connection established
- The Data transmitted to external server

Conclusion:

Network are analyzed to confirmed data exfiltration.

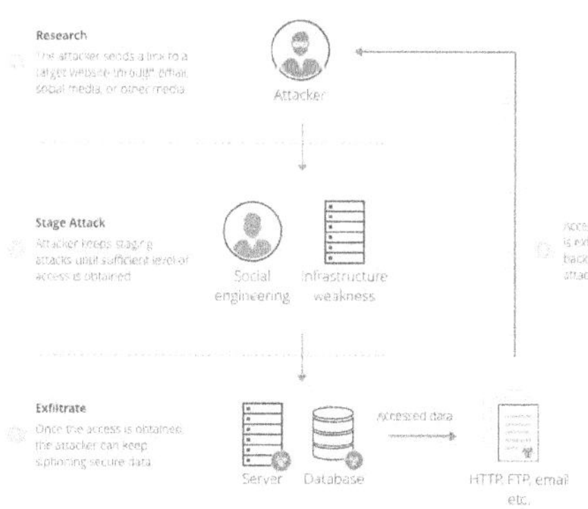

Figure 6.8: Network Attack Flow

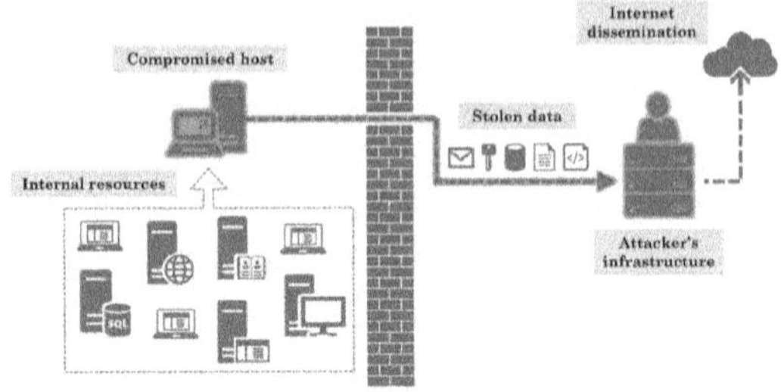

Fig 6.8: Data Exfiltration Attack Flow in a Compromised Network

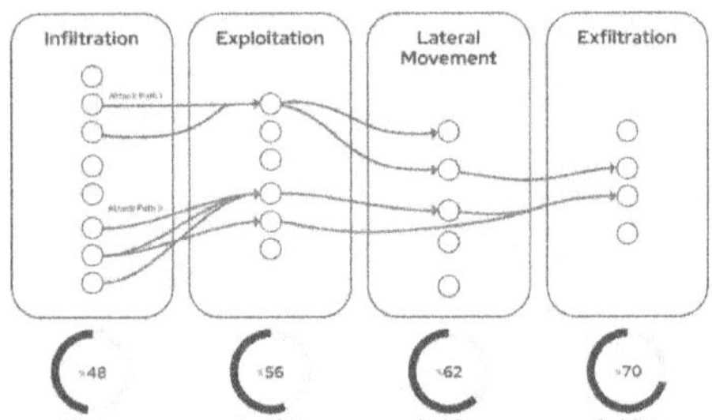

Fig 6.9: Cyber Attack Lifecycle: Infiltration, Exploitation, Lateral Movement and Exfiltration

PART B: MOBILE FORENSICS

6.8 The Introduction to Mobile Forensics

Mobile forensics are involving with the extraction and analyzing data from mobile devices such as smartphones, tablets, and from the wearable devices. In a simple terms, the mobile forensics are focused on collecting and examining the digital evidence that is stored in portable devices. It is an important because the smartphones, tablets, and wearable devices are very widely used in daily life and often can contain valuable information related to the communication, movement, and user activity.

In a practice, the investigators can extract data such as the call logs, text messages, emails, photos, videos, contacts, and browsing history, application records, and location details. This are the information that can help to reconstruct the events and to identify the connections between the people or incidents.

Mobile devices can contain valuable evidence such as:

- Messages
- Call logs
- Emails

- Location data
- App activity

6.9 The Challenges in Mobile Forensics

- Data encryption
- Device diversity
- Frequent OS updates
- Locked devices

6.10 Types of the Mobile Data

- Call logs
- SMS and chat messages
- Multimedia files
- Application data
- GPS/location data

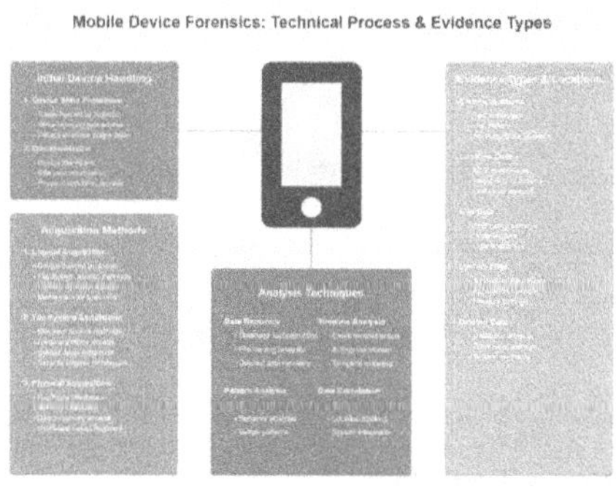

Figure 6.10: Mobile Data Sources

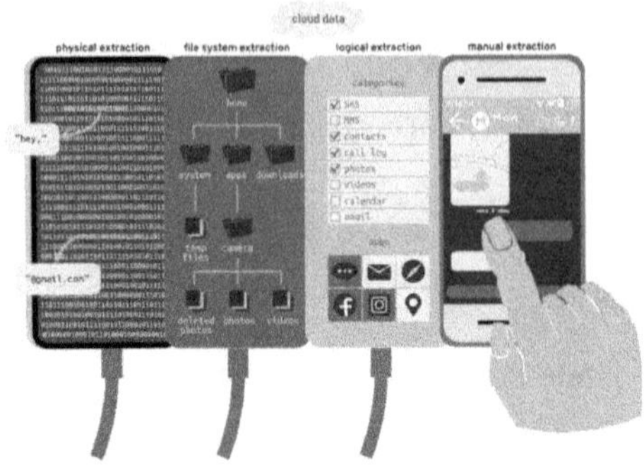

Fig 6.10: Mobile Device Data Extraction Methods: Physical, File System, Logical and Manual Extraction

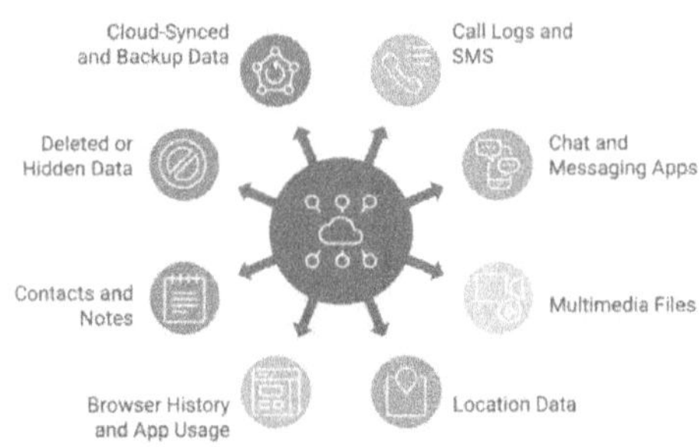

Fig 6.11: Types of Digital Evidence in Mobile Forensics

6.11 The Mobile Forensic Process

1. Seizure of device
2. Preservation
3. Data extraction
4. Analysis
5. Reporting

6.12 Mobile Data Extraction Techniques

1. Logical Extraction

- The Extracts that is accessible data
- Fast but it is limited

2. Physical Extraction

- The complete device copy
- Includes all the deleted data

3. File System Extraction

- Extracts the file system structure

6.13 Mobile Forensic Tools

Examples are include:

- Autopsy in the Digital Forensics Platform
- Specialized mobile tools like (Cellebrite, Oxygen — mention only academically)

The Mobile forensic tools are important because of the different devices and the operating systems that can store data in different formats. The Investigators often uses these tools to extract, decode, recover, and analyze the evidence from the smartphones and tablets in an organized by the manner.

In a practice, some of the tools are used for a general forensic analysis, while the others are specially that is designed for mobile devices. They may be helped to recover the deleted messages, and examine the application data, and analyze call records, extract media files, and it is generated for the investigation reports. The choice of the tools are often be depends on the device model, operating system version, and legal permissions are available in the case.

6.14 Case Study: Mobile Data Investigation

Scenario:

A suspect is been involved in fraud using mobile communication.

Investigation:

- To Extract call logs
- Analyze messages
- And Check app activity

Findings:

- For Suspicious communication
- To Transaction-related messages

Conclusion:

Mobile data are being provided critical evidence.

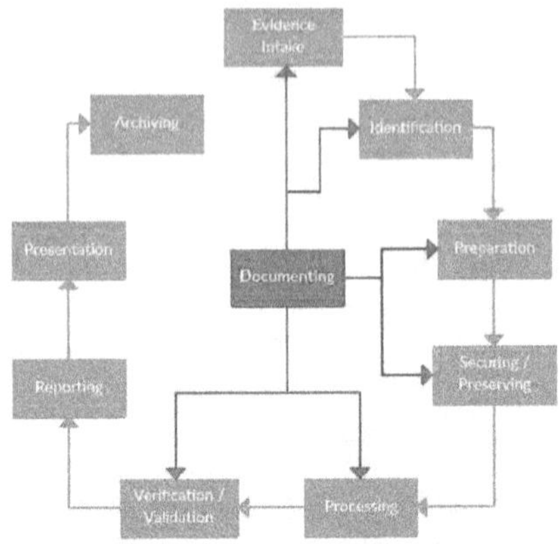

Figure 6.12: Mobile Investigation Flow

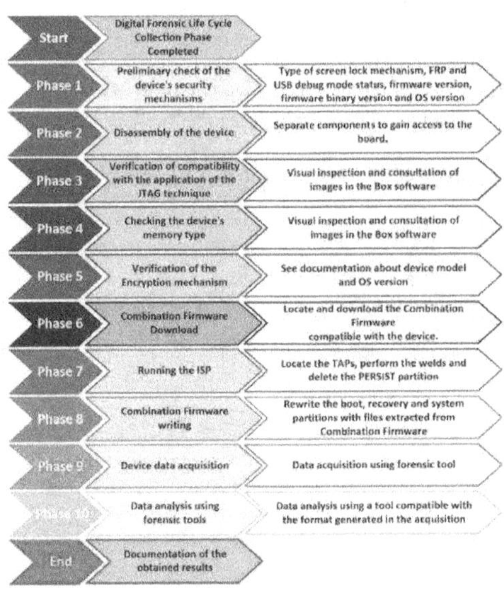

Fig 6.13: Mobile Device Forensic Investigation Life Cycle

6.15 Integration of Network and Mobile Forensics

Modern investigations often combine both domains.

Example:

- Mobile device used
- Data transmitted over network

The integration of the network and the mobile forensics is an important and because of many modern and the cyber incidents are involve in both the devices and the communication network are used by that device. Examining that only one side may be provide an incomplete view of the case. By combining both the domains, the investigators can understand the user actions as well as the related network activity.

In a practice, the evidence from a mobile phone such as the messages, app logs, browser activity, or stored files can be correlated are with the network evidence like the packet captures, server logs, IP addresses, and the connection records. This will helps to verify the timelines and identify communication between the devices and external systems.

6.16 Practical Lab: Network and Mobile Analysis

Objective:

Perform the basic network and mobile forensic analysis

Steps:

1. Capture network traffic
2. Analyze packets
3. Extract mobile data
4. Identify suspicious activity

Expected Outcome:

- Network behavior understood
- Mobile evidence identified

6.17 Key Points

- Network forensics analyzes communication
- Mobile forensics extracts personal data
- Both are critical in modern investigations
- Tools help reconstruct events

6.18 Summary

This chapter explored network and mobile forensics, highlighting their importance in modern cyber investigations. It is explained how the network traffic and the mobile data can be analyzed to detect and investigate the cybercrimes. The chapter also been discussed for an important concepts such as packet capture, network attack indicators, mobile data extraction, forensic tools, and the evidence analysis methods to use in practical investigations. These are the topics that shows how it is different sources of the digital evidence can be helped to reconstruct incidents and identify the suspicious activity.

Another the important point is that both domains should be present in a unique challenges, including encryption, the large data volumes, device diversity, and it is rapidly changing the technologies. The Investigators must therefore have to combine the technical knowledge with a proper forensic procedures to obtain the reliable results.

In many cases, the network and mobile evidence are closely connected and it should be examined together. Because of this, the understanding of both the network and mobile forensics is very essential for the effective digital for the investigations in the modern environment.

6.19 Review Questions

Short:

1. What is network forensics?
2. What is mobile forensics?

Long:

1. Explain packet analysis
2. Discuss mobile forensic techniques

6.20 Practical Exercise

A suspect is using a mobile device and internet connection for illegal activity.

- How will you investigate?
- What tools will you use?
- What evidence will you collect?

Multiple Choice Questions

1. Network forensics analyzes:
   A. Files
   B. Traffic
   C. RAM
   D. BIOS
   Answer: B
2. Packet is:
   A. File
   B. Data unit
   C. Log
   D. Program
   Answer: B
3. Protocol defines:
   A. Storage
   B. Communication rules
   C. Files
   D. RAM
   Answer: B
4. Wireshark captures:
   A. Files
   B. Packets
   C. Logs
   D. RAM
   Answer: B
5. Mobile forensics deals with:
   A. Servers
   B. Smartphones
   C. Routers
   D. BIOS
   Answer: B
6. Logical extraction:
   A. Full data
   B. Partial data
   C. RAM
   D. Logs
   Answer: B
7. Physical extraction:
   A. Partial
   B. Full copy
   C. Logs
   D. Cache
   Answer: B
8. Network indicator:
   A. Normal traffic

B. Unknown IP
C. Stable usage
D. Idle system
Answer: B

9. Mobile evidence includes:
A. Messages
B. Logs
C. Location
D. All
Answer: D

10. Session reconstruction:
A. Deletes data
B. Rebuilds communication
C. Encrypts data
D. Stores data
Answer: B

CHAPTER 7

Email and Web Forensics

7.1 Introduction

The Email and web-based communication both have become an essential components for the modern and digital interaction. However, they are also mostly among the commonly exploited mediums for the cybercrimes such as phishing, fraud, identity theft, and malware distribution.

Email forensics are mainly focuses on analyzing the email messages, headers, and transmission paths to identify the source and the authenticity of communication. The Web forensics, are on the other hand, it involves for examining a browser artifacts, web history, cookies, and cached data to reconstruct the user activity.

These are the two domains that are closely related because many cyber incidents involve both:

- Emails used as attack vectors
- Web browsers used to execute malicious actions

This chapter will provides a comprehensive understanding of the email and web forensic techniques, tools, and the real-world investigative approaches.

PART A: EMAIL FORENSICS

7.2 Concept of Email Forensics

Email forensics is the process of examining the email messages to:

- To Determine the origin of the message
- To Verify its authenticity
- To Identify any malicious intent
- Trace the sender

Every email has contains not only the visible to the content but also the hidden metadata that is known as email headers, which can provide crucial information about the message's journey.

7.3 Structure of an Email

An email is consists of two main components that are:

1. Header

It Contains metadata such as:

- The Sender address
- And Recipient address
- Date and time
- The Mail servers involved

2. Body

It Contains:

- The Message content
- The Attachments
- Embedded links

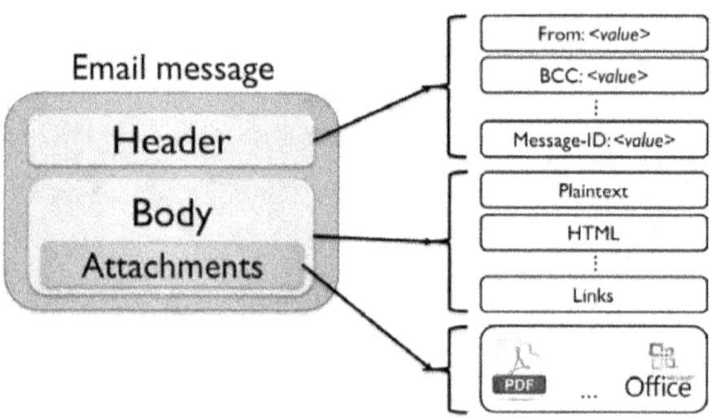

Figure 7.1: Email Structure

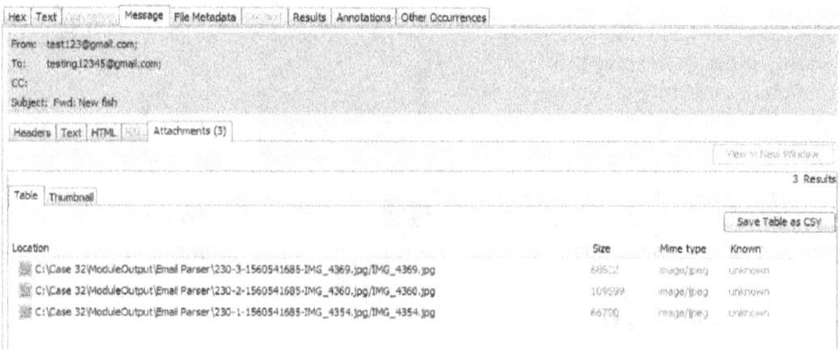

Fig 7.2: Email Evidence Analysis in Autopsy Digital Forensics Platform

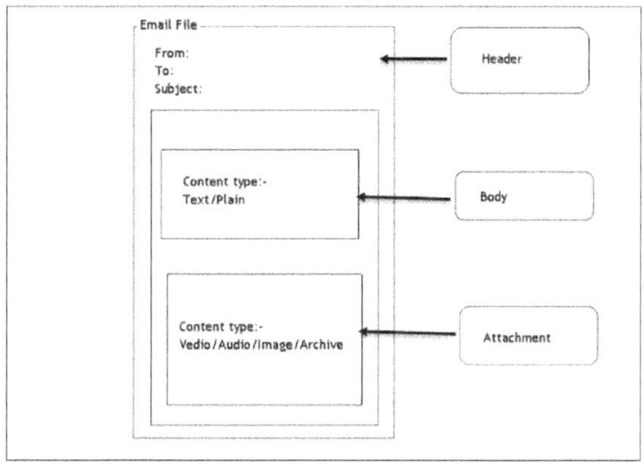

Fig 7.3: Structure of an Email Message (Header, Body, and Attachment)

7.4 Email Header Analysis

Email headers are the most important part of the email forensics. They are containing detailed routing information that will help to trace the origin of an email.

Key Header Fields:

- From → Sender address
- To → Recipient address
- Subject → Email topic
- Date → Time of sending
- Received → Mail servers through which the email passed
- Return-Path → Actual sending address

How Investigation Works:

- To Analyze "Received" fields from bottom to top
- To Identify originating IP address
- To Trace the server locations

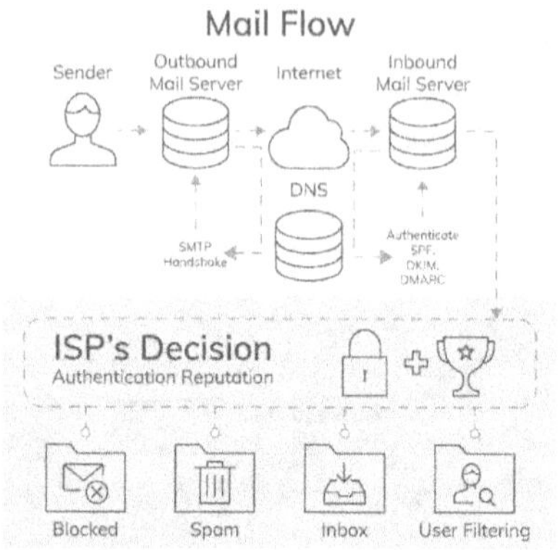

Figure 7.4: Email Routing Path

7.5 Common Email-Based Attacks

Email-based attacks are very common because the email is widely used for an personal, business, and official communications. Attackers are often use the email as an entry to point and to steal the information, spread malware, or trick the users into revealing the sensitive data. Because of this, email evidence is very highly relevant in many of the cyber investigations.

Common email-based attacks include phishing are spear phishing, spoofing, spam campaigns, and malware attachments, the business email compromise, and credential theft. Some of the attacks that is rely on fake links, while the others use of malicious documents or impersonated sender addresses to gain trust from the user, the common Email based Attacks are:

1. Phishing

Fake emails designed to steal sensitive information.

2. Spoofing

Forging sender identity to appear legitimate.

3. Malware Distribution

Emails containing malicious attachments or links.

4. Business Email Compromise (BEC)

Targeted attacks on organizations for financial fraud.

7.6 Email Forensic Techniques

Email forensic techniques are used to examine the suspicious emails and to identify their true source, purpose, and for the possible impact. These are the methods that helps the investigators to determine it whether an email is genuine, malicious, or part of a larger cyberattack.

In a practice, the header analysis is used to inspect the routing details, sender information, timestamps, and also the mail servers that is involved in delivery. IP tracing often helps to locate the origin of the message or to identify the suspicious network paths. Attachment analysis is performed to detect the hidden malware, malicious scripts, or harmful files. Link verification also checks it whether the embedded URLs lead to trusted websites or a fake phishing pages, The following Email Forensic Techniques are:

- The Header analysis
- IP tracing
- Attachment analysis
- Link verification
- Content examination

7.7 Case Study: Phishing Email Investigation

Scenario:

A user have received an email claiming to be from a bank and in the mail there is a link.

Investigation Steps:

1. To Analyze email header
2. To Identify sender IP
3. To Check link URL
4. Compare domain authenticity

Findings:

- The Email originated from suspicious IP
- Is it an Fake domain that is used

Conclusion:

Phishing attack confirmed

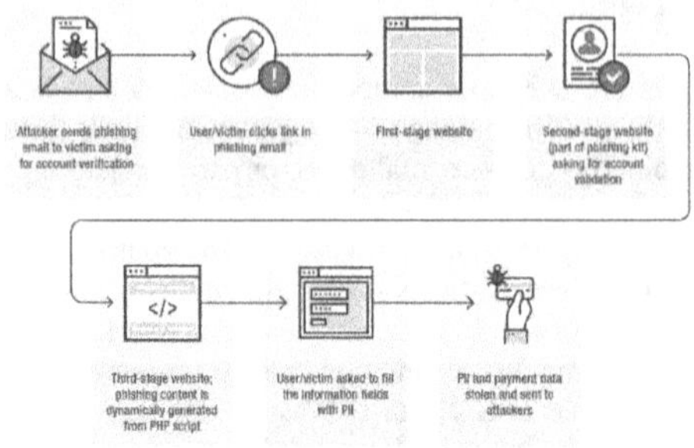

Figure 7.5: Phishing Attack Flow

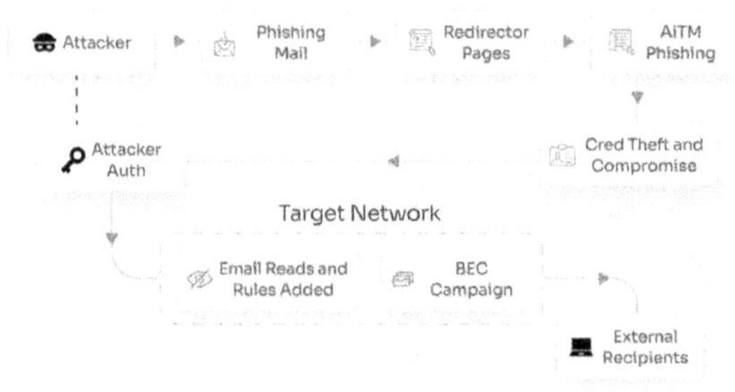

Fig 7.6: Advanced Phishing Attack Workflow and Credential Compromise Process

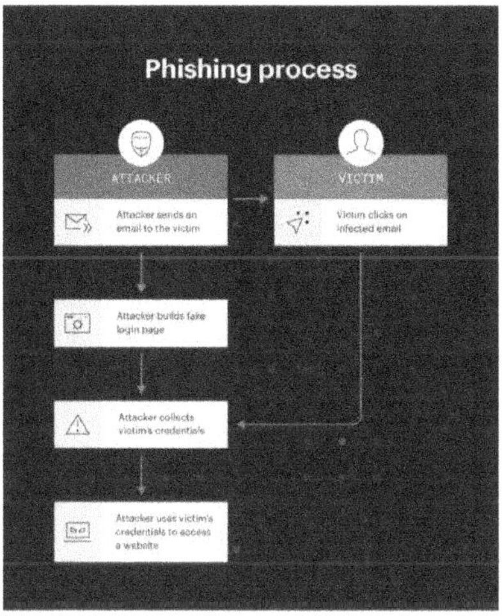

Fig 7.7: Basic Phishing Process and Credential Theft Flow

PART B: WEB FORENSICS

7.8 Introduction to Web Forensics

Web forensics involves to analyzing web browser data to understand user activity. In a simple terms, the web forensics it focuses on the examining the internet and the usage and its artifacts stored by the browsers and online applications. It is an important because the web browsers are very commonly used for the communication, searching, downloading files, financial transactions, and accessing the cloud services. These are the activities that often leaves a valuable traces on a system.

In a practice, the investigators analyze the browser history, cached files, cookies, and the saved passwords, bookmarks, download records, autofill data, and session information. This evidence can help to reconstruct that whether websites were visited, what actions are being performed, and when those actions had took place.

Browser history also can store large amounts of data such as:

- Browsing history
- Cookies
- Cache files

- Download history

This are the information that helps in investigators and reconstruct user actions.

7.9 Types of Browser Artifacts

1. Browsing History

List of the visited websites

2. Cookies

Small files that has used for storing session data

3. Cache

Temporary storage of that web content

4. Download Records

Details of the downloaded files

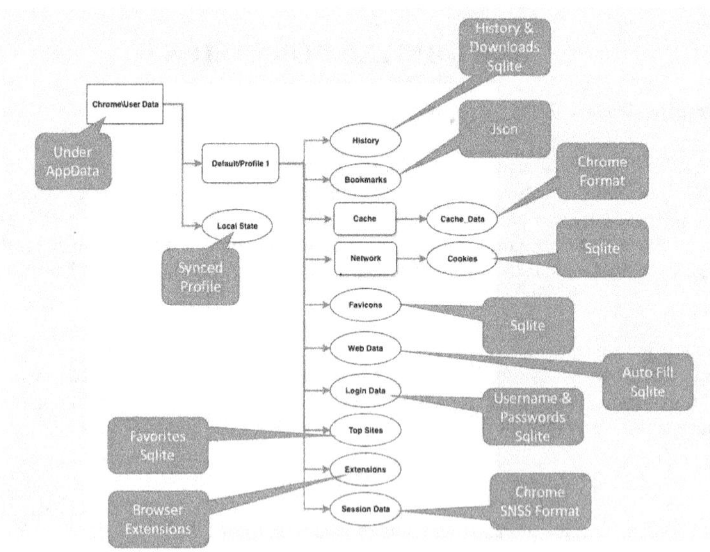

Figure 7.8: Browser Artifacts

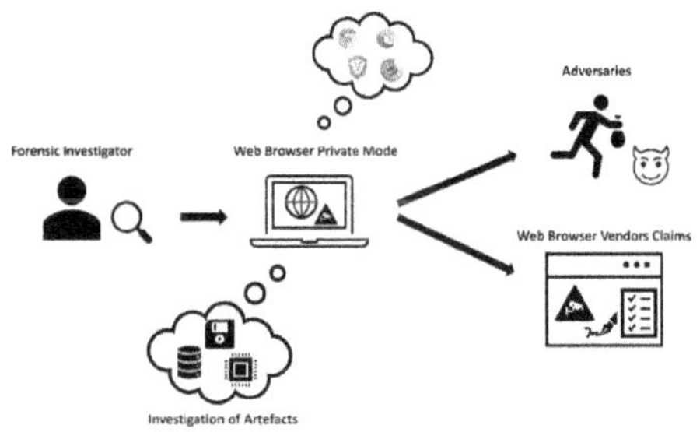

Fig 7.8: Web Browser Private Mode Forensics and Artifact Investigation

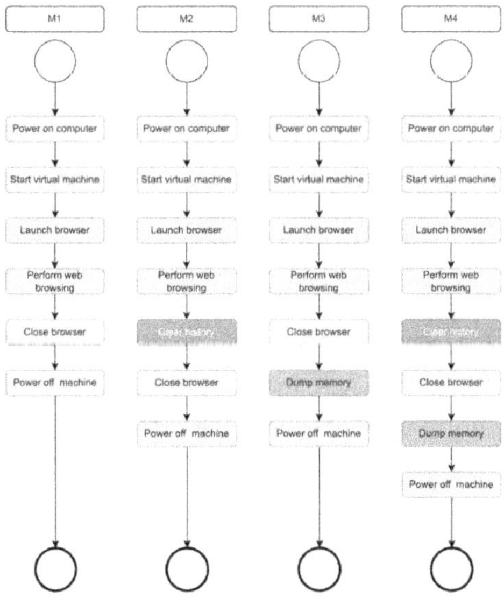

Fig 7.9: Web Browser Forensic Experiment Workflow and Evidence Collection Process

7.10 Importance of Web Forensics

Web forensics is important because the browsers are often used during the both normal activity and cyber incidents. Many of the actions are performed on the internet that can leave traces that will help the investigators to understand what user have done, when the activity happened, and whether the behavior was legitimate or it was suspicious.

In a practice, the web artifacts that are history files, cookies, cache records, downloads, saved sessions, and form the data that are examined to build a clear picture of the online behavior. These are the records may also support other evidence and its sources such as emails, system logs, or mobile data.

Web artifacts that help are:

- Track user activity
- Identify visited websites
- Detect malicious downloads
- Reconstruct attack sequences

7.11 Web Forensic Techniques

- History analysis
- Cookie examination
- Cache analysis
- Session reconstruction

7.12 Tools for Web Forensics

Tools that are include:

- The Autopsy Digital Forensics Platform
- The Browser-specific analysis tools

7.13 Case Study: Browser-Based Investigation

Scenario:

A system is been suspected of accessing the malicious websites.

Investigation:

- To Analyze browser history
- To Examine cookies
- To Check downloads

Findings:

- Suspicious websites visited
- Malware downloaded

Conclusion:

User activity confirmed the malicious intent

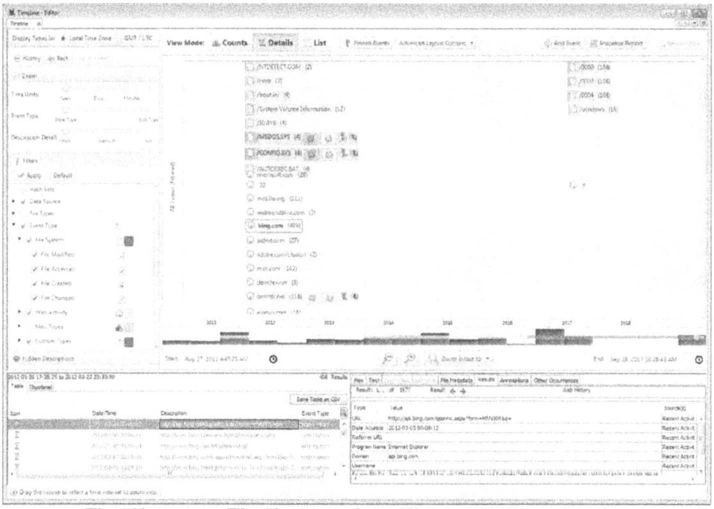

Fig 7.10: Autopsy Timeline Analysis for Web Activity Reconstruction

7.14 Integration of Email and Web Forensics

Many attacks are been combine for both domains:

Example:

- An Email contains malicious link
- To User clicks → browser opens
- To Malware downloaded

Both the email and the web evidence must be analyzed together

7.15 Practical Lab: Email and Web Investigation

Objective:

Analyze the email and browser data

Steps:

1. To Examine email header
2. To Identify sender IP
3. To Analyze browser history
4. To Detect malicious links

Expected Outcome:

- The Email source identified
- The User activity reconstructed

7.16 The Challenges in Email and Web Forensics

- For Encrypted communication
- For Anonymous email services
- The Private browsing modes
- And Data deletion

7.17 Key Points

- Email headers have reveal origin
- Web artifacts and its track activity
- Phishing is common attack
- Combined analysis make it powerful

7.18 Summary

This chapter provided a detailed understanding of email and web forensics. It explained how investigators analyze email headers and browser artifacts to detect cybercrimes and reconstruct user activity. Email attacks, and forensic techniques, like phishing investigation methods, private browsing artifacts, and the importance of the web evidence in digital cases. These are the topics that shows how communication data and its browser records can be reveal an important details during an investigation.

Another important point is that the email and web evidence are often support the other forensic sources such as system logs, network traffic, and mobile device data. When they are combined, they provide a clearer view of events and user behavior.

7.19 Review Questions

Short:

1. What is email forensics?
2. What is web forensics?

Long:

1. Explain email header analysis?
2. Discuss browser artifacts?

7.20 Practical Exercise

A user have received a suspicious email and clicks a link.

- How will you investigate?
- What evidence will you collect?
- What tools will you use?

Multiple Choice Questions

1. Email forensics analyzes:
   A. Files
   B. Emails
   C. RAM
   D. BIOS
   Answer: B
2. Email header contains:
   A. Content
   B. Metadata
   C. Images
   D. Files
   Answer: B
3. Phishing is:
   A. Protection
   B. Fraud attack
   C. Encryption
   D. Backup
   Answer: B
4. Spoofing means:
   A. Deletion
   B. Fake identity
   C. Encryption
   D. Backup
   Answer: B
5. Cookies store:
   A. Files
   B. Session data
   C. Logs
   D. RAM
   Answer: B
6. Cache stores:
   A. Temporary data
   B. Permanent data
   C. Logs
   D. RAM
   Answer: A
7. Browser history shows:
   A. Files
   B. Websites visited
   C. RAM
   D. Logs
   Answer: B
8. Header analysis helps:
   A. Delete email

B. Trace sender
C. Encrypt data
D. Store data
Answer: B

9. Web forensics analyzes:
A. Hardware
B. Browser artifacts
C. BIOS
D. RAM
Answer: B

10. Email attack includes:
A. Phishing
B. Spoofing
C. Malware
D. All
Answer: D

CHAPTER 8

Forensic Reporting and Documentation

8.1 Introduction

In the digital forensic investigations, the final and the most critical stage is presentation of the findings. No matter how strong is the evidence, it always holds a little value if it is not documented and reported it properly.

Forensic reporting is the process of its presenting the results of an investigation in a clear, structured, and should be acceptable in a legally manner. It will ensures that the technical findings can be understood by the non-technical individuals such as:

- The Judges
- The Lawyers
- The Law enforcement officers
- Organizational management

This chapter focuses on the principles, structure, and the importance of a forensic reporting and the documentation, and along with real-world practices.

8.2 The Importance of Forensic Reporting

Forensic reporting serves the multiple purposes:

- A Communicates investigation findings
- It should Provide legal evidence
- It Ensures transparency
- And Supports decision-making
- Maintains professional credibility

A well-prepared report can:

It will strengthen a case, and clearly explain technical evidence, Help in the legal proceedings

A poorly written report can:

Can Cause confusion, Lead to the rejection of the evidence, and it can Damage credibility

8.3 The Characteristics of a Good Forensic Report

A forensic report is a considered good when it is a clear, accurate, objective, and it should be easy to understand. It should present the findings in a professional manner so that the investigators, management, lawyers, or the court can review the results without a confusion. The report must be explained what was been examined, how is the examination was performed, and what conclusions were reached to.

In a practice, a good forensic report should be a well-organized, fact-based, and it is free from unnecessary assumptions. And in the Technical terms it may be used when it is required, but they should be explained in a simple language whenever it is possible. Supporting a details such as screenshots, logs, timestamps, hash values, and the references to evidence should also be included where relevant

A high-quality forensic report must be having the following characteristics:

1. Clarity

The report that should be an easy to understand and avoid unnecessary technical jargon.

2. Accuracy

All the information and it must be correct and it is based on verified evidence.

3. Completeness

The report it should be include all relevant findings and procedures.

4. Objectivity

The investigator must be remain neutral and avoid personal opinions.

5. Consistency

The report it should be followed as structured format.

8.4 Structure of a Forensic Report

The structure of a forensic report is very important and because the information must be presented in a logical and a consistent order. A well-structured report helps the readers to quickly understand the background of the case, the examination process, findings, and final conclusions. It will also make the future review make it easier when the report is revisited.

In a practice, the common sections may be included the case information, objectives, evidence received, tools used, methodology, and examination steps, findings, screenshots or supporting artifacts, conclusion, and the recommendations. Some of the reports may also be include for appendices for logs, hash values, chain of custody records, or detailed a technical results, and the standard forensic report and typically includes the following sections:

1. Title Page

- The Case name
- The Investigator name
- Date and Time

2. Introduction

- The Purpose of investigation
- The Scope of analysis

3. Case Background

- To Description of incident
- To Context of investigation

4. Methodology

- Tools used
- Procedures followed
- Acquisition methods

5. The Evidence Description

- A List of collected evidence
- Details of devices

6. Analysis and Findings

- The Results of investigation
- Observations

7. Conclusion

- The Summary of findings

8. Recommendations

- To Preventive measures

9. Appendices

- Logs
- Screenshots
- Supporting data

Figure 8.1: Forensic Report Structure

8.5 Documentation in Digital Forensics

Documentation begins and from the first stage of an investigation and it continues to until the final report is completed. It is an important a because and every action and it is taken during the case and may need to be reviewed, verified, or explained later. And it Clear the records to help maintain transparency and accountability.

In a practice, the documentation and may include the evidence of collection details, dates and times, tools used, acquisition methods, analyst observations, screenshots, extracted data, hash values, and the decisions that made during the analysis. Even a small steps can become important when it is reconstructing the investigation process.

Documentation is a continuous process to throughout the investigation.

Includes:

- For the Evidence collection details
- Chain of custody records
- All Tools and techniques used
- Observations and notes

Proper documentation that ensures:

- The Reproducibility
- The Transparency
- Legal validity

8.6 The Maintaining Investigation Notes

Investigators must maintain a detailed notes including:

- Date and time of actions
- System details
- Commands executed
- Observations

These are the notes to help in:

- Writing reports
- Verifying results
- Supporting testimony

8.7 Legal Considerations in Reporting

Legal compliance is a important and because the forensic reports may be presented in the court, internal disciplinary and proceedings, or official investigations. A report is that does not follow a legal standards and may be challenged, rejected, or given less evidentiary and valued. Because of this, the reporting must be prepared with the accuracy and professionalism.

In a practice, the reports should be an objective, fact-based, and free from a personal bias. They must clearly describe the evidence and examined, methods used, limitations of the analysis, and conclusions to support by findings. And the Confidential information should be handled carefully, and it is authorized procedures and must be followed during the evidence collection and examination.

Forensic reports must comply with the legal standards.

Key Aspects:

- The Evidence must be admissible
- Procedures must follow legal guidelines
- And the Chain of custody must be maintained
- And Expert testimony may be required

8.8 The Common Mistakes in Forensic Reporting

- And Using the excessive technical language
- Missing important details
- Lack of proper structure
- Incomplete documentation
- Drawing unsupported conclusions

Avoiding these mistakes and it is essential for professional reporting.

8.9 Case Study: Preparing a Forensic Report

Scenario:

A system was being investigated for data theft.

Investigation Summary:

- Disk image created
- Deleted files recovered
- USB activity identified

Report Writing Steps:

1. Describe case background
2. Document tools used
3. Present findings
4. Provide conclusion

Outcome:

A clear and structured report will helped and establish evidence in the case.

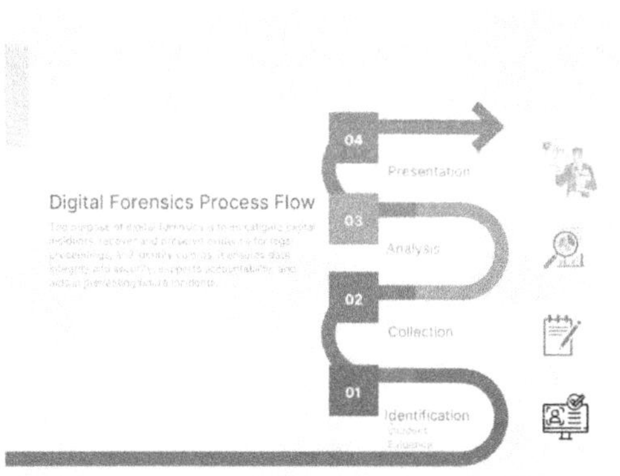

Figure 8.2: Reporting Workflow

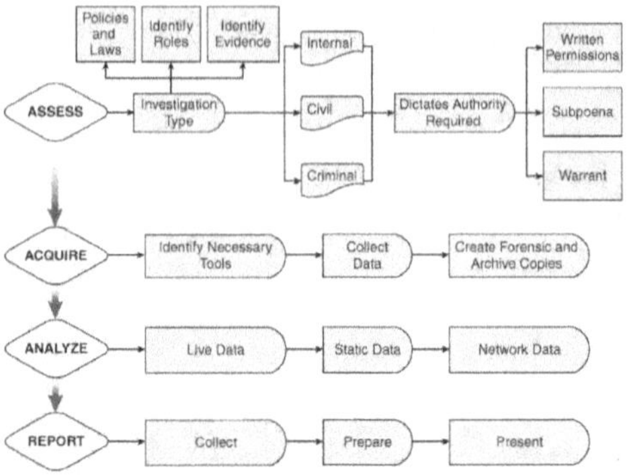

Fig 8.1: Digital Forensic Investigation and Reporting Process Flow

8.10 Writing Style for Forensic Reports

- To Use simple and clear language
- And Avoid assumptions
- Present facts logically
- To Use bullet points where necessary
- Include diagrams and tables

8.11 Practical Lab: Writing a Forensic Report

Objective:

Prepare a forensic report based on the investigation findings.

Steps:

1. To Collect investigation data
2. Organize findings
3. Write structured report
4. Review for accuracy

Expected Outcome:

- Clear and professional report
- Proper documentation
-

8.12 Key Points

- For Reporting is the final stage of investigation
- And Clear communication is essential
- Documentation supports evidence
- Legal compliance is necessary
- The Structure improves readability

8.13 Summary

The chapter also be discussed and key qualities of a good forensic report, and continuous documentation practices, and the legal considerations and that must be followed during the reporting. These are elements are helped to ensure that the findings are reliable, understandable, and it is professionally presented.

Another the important point is that the reporting is not only the final stage of an investigation, but also a bridge between the technical analysis and decision-making. To clear reports allow the investigators, organizations, and courts to understand its complex digital evidence more easily.

This is a chapter that explained the importance of a forensic reporting and the documentation. It is highlighted how to structure reports, and maintain investigation records, the present findings in a clear and legally acceptable manner in the court.

8.14 Review Questions

Short:

1. What is forensic reporting?
2. Why is documentation important?

Long:

1. Explain structure of forensic report?
2. Discuss legal aspects of reporting?

8.15 Practical Exercise

You completed a forensic investigation.

- How will you prepare the report?
- What sections will you include?
- How will you ensure clarity and accuracy?

Multiple Choice Questions

1. Forensic reporting is:
   A. Data deletion
   B. Documentation
   C. Encryption
   D. Storage
   Answer: B
2. Report must be:
   A. Complex
   B. Clear
   C. Hidden
   D. Short
   Answer: B
3. Documentation ensures:
   A. Speed
   B. Transparency
   C. Storage
   D. Encryption
   Answer: B
4. Report includes:
   A. Findings
   B. Tools
   C. Methodology
   D. All
   Answer: D
5. Accuracy means:
   A. Correct data
   B. Fast
   C. Short
   D. Encrypted
   Answer: A
6. Objectivity means:
   A. Opinion
   B. Neutrality
   C. Bias
   D. Guess
   Answer: B
7. Poor report causes:
   A. Strong case
   B. Rejection
   C. Better result
   D. Fast process
   Answer: B
8. Notes include:
   A. Time
   B. Tools
   C. Actions
   D. All
   Answer: D

9. Legal compliance ensures:
   A. Speed
   B. Admissibility
   C. Storage
   D. Encryption
   Answer: B
10. Report audience includes:
   A. Judges
   B. Lawyers
   C. Management
   D. All
   Answer: D

CHAPTER 9

Advanced Topics in Digital Forensics

9.1 Introduction

Digital forensics is constantly evolving and due to the rapid advancements with the technology. That the Old ways the forensic methods are focused mainly on the computers and storage devices. However, the modern investigations are now involve in the cloud platforms, volatile memory, artificial intelligence, and emerging technologies.

This chapter also introduces and advanced areas of the digital forensics that are becoming an increasingly importance in the real-world investigations. While these topics may go beyond the basic concepts, but they will provide a strong foundation for the future learning and professional growth.

9.2 Cloud Forensics

9.2.1 What is Cloud Forensics?

Cloud forensics are involves the collection, preservation, and analysis of data that stored in cloud environments such as:

- The Google Drive
- Dropbox
- AWS servers

Unlike the traditional systems, the data is in the cloud is:

- To Distributed across multiple locations
- And Managed by third-party providers
- Often encrypted

Figure 9.1: Cloud Forensics Architecture

9.2.2 The Challenges in Cloud Forensics

- Lack of the physical access
- Data spread across the locations
- Legal jurisdiction are an issues
- The Multi-user environments

9.2.3 Evidence Sources in Cloud

- All the Cloud logs
- The User activity records
- A Virtual machine snapshots
- The Email services

9.2.4 Importance

Cloud forensics is critical because most of it are modern applications that rely on the cloud infrastructure.

9.3 Memory Forensics

9.3.1 What is Memory Forensics?

In a simple terms, the memory forensics are focuses on examining the data that is existed only while a computer or device is running. All the data is stored in Random Access Memory (RAM) and may be disappear when the system is shut down or restarted. Because of this, the RAM can contain valuable and the evidence that is not available from the disk analysis alone.

In a practice, the investigators are capture a memory the image from the live system and analyze it using the specialized forensic tools. The analysis that it may reveal the running processes, an active network and connections, logged-in users, command history, loaded drivers, encryption keys, clipboard data, and traces of the malware activity.

Memory forensics that involves analyzing the volatile memory (RAM) to extract the information that is lost when a system is powered off.

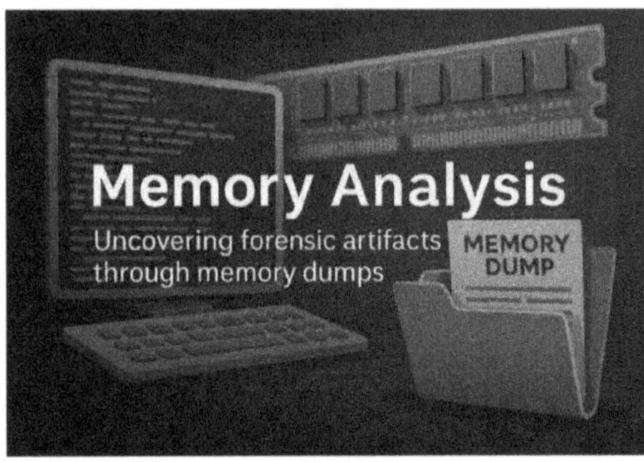

Figure 9.2: Memory Forensics Concept

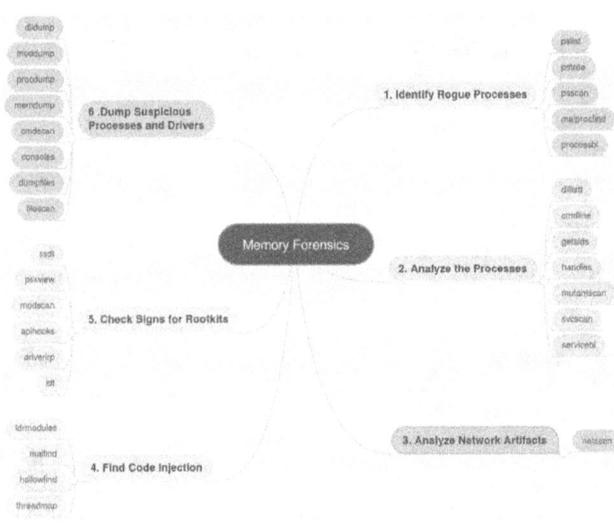

Fig 9.3: Memory Forensics Investigation Techniques and Analysis Workflow

9.3.2 What it can Be Found in RAM?

- The Running processes
- The Open network connections
- Encryption keys
- Malware artifacts

9.3.3 Importance

Memory forensics is useful in followings:

- To Detecting advanced malware
- To Investigating live attacks
- To Recovering hidden processes

9.3.4 Challenges

- The Data is temporary
- That Requires live acquisition
- Complex analysis

9.4 Artificial Intelligence in Digital Forensics

9.4.1 The Role of AI

Artificial Intelligence rapidly increasingly and used in digital forensics to:

- Automate the data analysis
- Detect the anomalies
- Identify the patterns

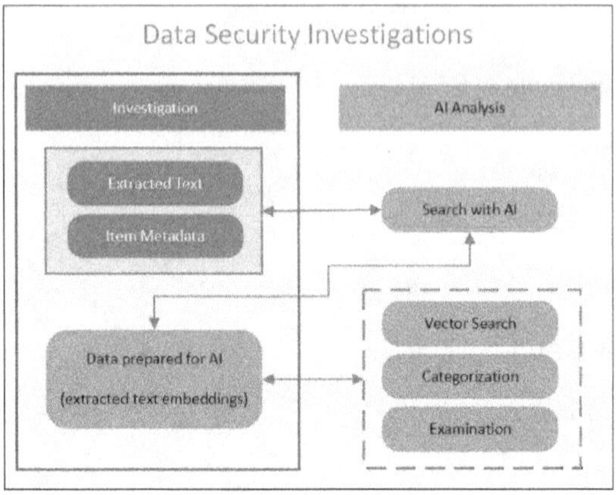

Figure 9.4: AI in Forensics

9.4.2 Applications

- For Malware detection
- For Image and video analysis
- Log analysis
- Fraud detection

9.4.3 Advantages

- For Faster analysis
- Handles large datasets
- Improves accuracy

9.4.4 Limitations

- To Requires training data
- Risk of false positives
- Lack of transparency

9.5 IoT Forensics (Internet of Things)

9.5.1 Concept

IoT forensics are also involves to analyzing the data from smart devices such as:

- The Smart home devices
- And Wearables
- Smart cameras

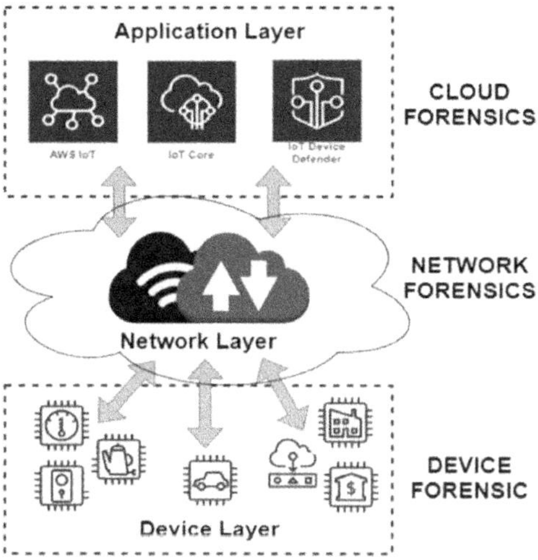

Figure 9.5: IoT Forensics Environment

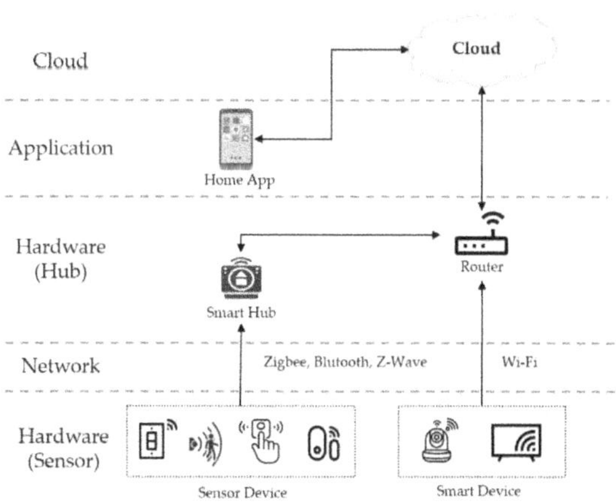

Fig 9.6: IoT Device Architecture and Cloud Communication Model

9.5.2 The Evidence Sources

- Device logs
- Sensor data
- Network communication

9.5.3 The Challenges

- Device diversity
- Limited storage
- Lack of standardization

9.6 Future Trends in Digital Forensics

The Digital forensics is a continuously evolving. Some of the important future trends include:

- A Cloud-native investigations
- AI-driven analysis
- A Block chain forensics
- Quantum computing impact
- Automated forensic systems

9.7 Case Study: Cloud-Based Data Breach

Scenario:

An organization that experiences a data breach in its cloud storage.

Investigation:

- To Analyze cloud logs
- To Identify unauthorized access
- To Trace user activity

Findings:

- The Suspicious login detected
- Data downloaded

Conclusion:

Cloud forensic and the analysis helped to identify the breach source.

9.8 Practical Lab (Conceptual)

Objective:

Understand the advanced of forensic concepts

Tasks:

- To Identify cloud evidence sources

- To Analyze memory artifacts (conceptually)
- Discuss AI applications

9.9 The Key Points

- The Cloud forensics deals with distributed data
- Memory forensics analyzes volatile data
- The AI enhances forensic capabilities
- IoT introduces new challenges
- Future trends shape investigations

9.10 Summary

The chapter also showed that the digital investigations are been continuously evolving with the changes in technology. The Traditional forensic methods will remain important, but new the environments such as the cloud platforms, smart devices, and memory-based attacks require a updated skills and tools.

Another the important point is that the advanced forensic areas are often involve for the challenges such as the encryption, distributed data storage, volatile evidence, privacy concerns, and large-scale and data analysis. The Investigators must therefore be combine with the technical knowledge with a proper legal and procedural understanding.

This chapter is introduced in a advanced topics in the digital forensics, including cloud forensics, memory analysis, AI applications, and IoT investigations. These areas are represent the future of forensic science and are essential for the handling modern cyber threats.

9.11 Review Questions

Short:

1. What is cloud forensics?
2. What is memory forensics?

Long:

1. Explain role of AI in digital forensics?
2. Discuss challenges in IoT forensics?

9.12 Practical Exercise

A cyber incident involves cloud storage and mobile devices.

- What advanced techniques will you use?
- What challenges will you face?
- How will you handle evidence?

REFERENCES

Casey, E. (2011). *Digital Evidence and Computer Crime* (3rd ed.). Academic Press.

Carrier, B. (2005). *File System Forensic Analysis*. Addison-Wesley.

Mandia, K., Prosise, C., & Pepe, M. (2014). *Incident Response and Computer Forensics* (3rd ed.). McGraw-Hill.

Sammons, J. (2012). *The Basics of Digital Forensics*. Elsevier.

Altheide, C., & Carvey, H. (2011). *Digital Forensics with Open Source Tools*. Syngress.

Marrington, A. (2010). *Digital Forensics: Digital Evidence in Criminal Investigations*. Wiley.

Behl, N. (2017). *Digital Forensics and Cyber Crime Investigation*. BPB Publications.

Singh, R. K. (2019). *Cyber Forensics Fundamentals*. Khanna Publishing.

National Institute of Standards and Technology. (2006).
Guide to Integrating Forensic Techniques into Incident Response (SP 800-86).

National Institute of Standards and Technology. (2014).
Guidelines on Mobile Device Forensics (SP 800-101 Rev.1).

National Institute of Standards and Technology.
Guide to Computer Security Log Management (SP 800-92).

EC-Council.
Computer Hacking Forensic Investigator (CHFI) Study Guide. Latest Edition.

Centre for Development of Advanced Computing.
Digital Forensics and Cyber Security Training Material.

SANS Institute.
Digital Forensics and Incident Response Resources.

International Organization on Computer Evidence.
Guidelines for Best Practices in Digital Evidence Collection.

Beebe, N. L., & Clark, J. G. (2005). A hierarchical, objectives-based framework for digital investigations. *Digital Investigation Journal*.

Quick, D., & Choo, K. K. R. (2014). Digital forensic intelligence: Data subsets and open source intelligence. *Future Generation Computer Systems*.

Garfinkel, S. (2010). Digital forensics research: The next 10 years. *Digital Investigation.*

Sommer, P. (2004). Digital evidence and computer crime. *International Journal of Digital Evidence.*

Scarfone, K., & Mell, P.
Guide to Network Forensics. NIST.

Hoog, A. (2011). *Android Forensics.* Elsevier.

Zdziarski, J. (2008). *iPhone Forensics.* O'Reilly Media.

Ruan, K. (2013). Cloud forensics. *IEEE Security & Privacy.*

Pearson, S. (2013). Cloud security and privacy. *IEEE.*

Roussev, V. (2010). Memory forensics techniques. *Digital Investigation.*

Spafford, E. H. (2018). Artificial intelligence in cybersecurity. *IEEE Security.*

Wang, Y. (2017). Machine learning in digital forensics. *Elsevier.*

Atzori, L., Iera, A., & Morabito, G. (2010). The Internet of Things: A survey. *IEEE Communications Magazine.*

Sicari, S., Rizzardi, A., Grieco, L., & Coen-Porisini, A. (2015). Security and privacy in IoT. *Elsevier.*

ISO/IEC 27037.
Guidelines for Identification, Collection, Acquisition, and Preservation of Digital Evidence.

ISO/IEC 27042.
Guidelines for Analysis and Interpretation of Digital Evidence.

APPENDIX

Appendix A: Sample Forensic Report

Case Title:

Unauthorized Data Access Investigation

Case ID:

DF-2026-001

Investigator:

Ronaldo Deka

Date:

10 April 2026

1. Introduction

This report is to represents the findings of a digital forensic investigation and been conducted on a computer system for suspected of the unauthorized data access and the file deletion.

2. Scope of Investigation

The investigation are focused on:

- To Identifying unauthorized access
- To Recovering deleted files
- Analyzing system activity

3. Evidence Collected

- Laptop (Windows OS)
- USB storage device
- Disk image file

4. Tools Used

- FTK Imager
- Autopsy Digital Forensics Platform

5. Methodology

1. For Evidence acquisition using forensic imaging
2. Hash verification
3. Analysis of disk image
4. Recovery of deleted files

6. Findings

- Confidential files accessed at unusual time
- USB device connected during activity
- Files deleted shortly after

7. Conclusion

The investigation confirms unauthorized access and data transfer.

8. Recommendations

- Implement access control policies
- Monitor USB usage
- Conduct regular audits

Appendix B: Chain of Custody Form

Case Details

Field	Description
Case ID	DF-2026-001
Case Title	Data Theft Investigation
Investigator	Ronaldo Deka

Table 10.1: Sample Case Information for a Forensic Report

Evidence Details

Evidence ID	Description	Location
E-01	Laptop	Office
E-02	USB Drive	Lab

Table 10.2: Sample Evidence Inventory Register

Chain of Custody Record

Date	Time	Person	Action	Signature
10/04/2026	10:00 AM	Investigator A	Collected	______
10/04/2026	11:30 AM	Analyst B	Received	______
10/04/2026	02:00 PM	Lab Officer	Stored	______

Table 10.3: Sample Chain of Custody Record

Note:

- To Every transfer must be recorded
- And Signatures are mandatory
- Maintain secure storage

Appendix C: Tool Installation Guide

1. Installing FTK Imager

Steps:

1. To Download from official website
2. To Run installer
3. To Follow setup instructions
4. Launch application

Requirements:

- Windows OS
- Minimum 4GB RAM

2. Installing Autopsy Digital Forensics Platform

Steps:

1. To Download Autopsy installer
2. To Install Java (if required)
3. To Run setup
4. To Launch and create first case

3. Installing Wireshark

Steps:

1. To Download from official site
2. To Install with default settings
3. To Install packet capture driver (Npcap)
4. To Start capturing network traffic

Precautions During Installation

- Download only from official sources
- Avoid pirated versions
- Ensure system compatibility

Publisher: Eliva Press Global Ltd

Email: info@elivapress.com

Eliva Press is an independent international publishing house established for the publication and dissemination of academic works all over the world. Company provides high quality and professional service for all of our authors.

Our Services:

Free of charge, open-minded, eco-friendly, innovational.

-Free standard publishing services (manuscript review, step-by-step book preparation, publication, distribution, and marketing).

-No financial risk. The author is not obliged to pay any hidden fees for publication.

-Editors. Dedicated editors will assist step by step through the projects.

-Money paid to the author for every book sold. Up to 50% royalties guaranteed.

-ISBN (International Standard Book Number). We assign a unique ISBN to every Eliva Press book.

-Digital archive storage. Books will be available online for a long time. We don't need to have a stock of our titles. No unsold copies. Eliva Press uses environment friendly print on demand technology that limits the needs of publishing business. We care about environment and share these principles with our customers.

-Cover design. Cover art is designed by a professional designer.

-Worldwide distribution. We continue expanding our distribution channels to make sure that all readers have access to our books.

-Marketing tools. We provide marketing tools such as banners, paid advertising, social media promotion and more.